Harry Dobermann – after an early career in the toy industry and psychic research, Harry moved into the fledgling world of computers and managed to be one of the few people not to make any money out of it.

Interested in Film, TV and Comics he runs The Patrick Wymark Boardroom website dedicated to the star of The Plane Makers and The Power Game.

BEYOND THE BORDERS OF FEAR brings together a selection of writings on film, TV and books including the controversial article, "The Destiny of Doctor Who – An Adventure in Time and Trainspotting."

BEYOND THE BORDERS OF FEAR

First published in Great Britain by Scatola Publishing

Copyright © 2021 by Harry Dobermann

ISBN 978-0-9570845-2-0

Harry Dobermann

Beyond the Borders of Fear

Contents

Introduction: Where The Shadows Freeze

"But surely," you say, "this is just a bunch of articles and reviews stuck together?" And in a very literal sense you are right. But, if you're old enough to remember the days of television sets with valves in the back, you may recall that moment when you switched off the set and the light gradually contracted to a dwindling star in the centre of the screen. And sometimes, around the edges, were the frozen shadows of the actors.

In those days when TV habitually closed down around midnight, didn't you wonder if those frozen shadows were stored somewhere? In the valves or in the ether? We thought those TV shows were lost forever. But if you could just connect a few wires and transistors to the back of the set, maybe you could recall them, to watch again

Today, everything is available on demand. Videotapes were superseded by DVD's and even that solid medium is being replaced by streaming – a literal realisation of that fantasy of recalling the frozen shadows. The audience is changing too. Forty years ago, an interest in anything old or fantastical was something to be hidden away as a secret. Today, commercialisation has lent those interests a sort of respectability.

But, I'm an unrepentant analogue guy. And this is my own personal streaming platform, where I'm indulging myself by unfreezing some of my favourite shadows. It includes the article, "The Destiny of Doctor Who – An Adventure in Time and Trainspotting" because I was advised that it might be culturally significant to have an article about "Doctor Who" in the collection. But feel free to skip over it. Towards the end, there are some reviews of books about the real world. The final piece is a memoir of my short career as a 'ghost hunter'. Again, something from the analogue world, but worth recording, I hope.

In conclusion, I hope you enjoy this book. If you do, or even if you don't, please drop it off at your local charity shop when you've finished with it.

The Destiny of Doctor Who – An Adventure in Time and Trainspotting

Black Orchid is an episode of the *Doctor Who* TV show best watched with the audio commentary turned on so that you can hear the star Peter Davison reminding us that it's crap. Nevertheless, when Doctor Who (the character) reveals that as a boy* he always wanted to drive a steam train, he nails the hidden destiny of *Doctor Who*.

in view of recent developments within the reality of the tv show, feel free to substitute whichever gender you think is appropriate here

In the same way that British Railways was the state-owned railway operator between 1948 and 1997, the British Broadcasting Corporation is the British public service broadcaster, established under Royal Charter in 1927. In 1955, British Rail began a programme of modernisation, replacing steam engines with new diesel locomotives. Six years later, the BBC hired Sydney Newman, to reinvigorate its drama output. *Dr Who* was one of Newman's innovations.

In 1942, Ian Allan , a clerk in the Southern Railway publicity section at Waterloo had responded to increasing requests for information by publishing the 'ABC of Southern Locomotives'. This led to a series of booklets covering all regions of the United Kingdom, and in 1945, he left Southern Railway to set up Ian Allan Publishing . The company would become the world's leading transport publisher. Allan also set up the 'locospotters club' , marshalling the ad hoc pastime into a community of 230,000 members pledging not to trespass or misbehave on railway property.

In 1965, the *William (Dr Who) Hartnell Fan Club* was created, rejuvenating into the *Doctor Who Fan Club* in 1967. The original fan club was encouraged and financially supported by the BBC up until the Tom Baker era, when it was superseded by the independent *Doctor Who Appreciation Society*. Membership of the *DWAS* appears to have been on a much smaller scale than the 'locospotters club' – a membership of three thousand being only a fraction of the potential audience - Virgin books would print and sell around 25,000 copies of each novelisation and home video cassettes sold between 20,000 and 50,000 copies.*

In 1963, physicist and engineer Dr Richard Beeching of the British Transport Commission, published a report which advocated addressing falling revenue by cutting a third of passenger services and over half the existing train stations. The proposals were opposed by both unions and the rail travelling public. In 1985, BBC1 controller Michael Grade reacted to falling viewing figures by proposing the cancellation of Doctor Who. In response to public outrage, the series was at first "rested" and returned after 18 months with a new lead actor. It was finally "not-renewed" in 1989.

With the 1955 modernisation plan replacing steam with diesel and electric locomotives, and lines being closed as a result of the 1963 Beeching report, a new breed of enthusiast emerged to preserve what was disappearing. These enthusiasts were not content just to record facts about the trains. They wanted to *drive the trains*. And they wanted to maintain the trains and preserve the lines. *The Bluebell Line* – opened in 1960 – was the UK's first standard gauge (i.e. full size) passenger railway, run by volunteers and reopening part of the Lewes to East Grinstead Line. Today, millions travel on our preserved railways. Many would not consider themselves locospotters or enthusiasts. The preserved railways are just another industry open to the public.

With *Doctor Who* no longer supported as TV show, it became similar to a redundant train line. Enthusiasts now ran the show. In 1989, Virgin Books had exhausted most of the TV episodes which could be novelised and negotiated the rights to publish original novels. These had more adult themes and a greater imaginative reach than what had been appearing on TV. In 1999, the audio company *Big Finish* produced an original full-cast *Doctor Who* adventure *The Sirens of Time*. This company became very much the equivalent of a Railway Preservation Society. They employed former *Doctor Who* actors in the same way that the early preserved lines employed former railwaymen to use their skills. Doubtless if things had gone differently, *Big Finish* would have become the official successor to the BBC in preserving the heritage of *Dr Who*.

But the BBC began to realize that – while *Dr Who* had no value as a TV show – it was a valuable merchandising property. As Miles Booy put it in 2012*, *"a fan born in the late 60s... has been collecting sets of Doctor Who in some format (novelisations, video, DVD) for literally as long as they could remember. T.S. Eliot's Prufrock counted out his life in teaspoons – I've spent mine waiting for The Sun Makers to come out."*

This reflects the experience of railway enthusiasts. As Nicholas Whittaker notes** *"At the serious end of the collecting business a stout chequebook is essential"*

In 1993 Virgin proposed to formalise the continuation of TV Doctor into book Doctor with a regeneration into a new doctor "played" (on book covers and personal appearances) by David Troughton. The BBC vetoed it. In 1996 they licensed a film to be made by Universal for the Fox network and the BBC starring Stephen McGann and in 1997 the BBC took back publishing of the New Adventures. Ironically, in 2005 the BBC brought back *Doctor Who* as a TV show under iconoclastic writer-producer Russell T Davies.

*-Miles Booy, Love and Monsters:The Doctor Who Experience 1979 to the Present – I.B.Tauris & Co, 2012

**- Nicholas Whittaker Platform Souls: The Trainspotter as 20th Century Hero, Icon Books 2015 (Gollancz 1995)

This new series strongly reflected the approach of the Virgin New Adventures. As Miles Booy puts it, *"Who products which had been precision exercises in niche marketing in the 1990s now constituted a massive Research and Development Division for what became a massive mainstream hit."*

More than this – the new *Dr Who* was written, directed, produced and acted in by former fans (most prominently Peter Capaldi – fanzine writer in the 1970's and Dr Who himself in the 21st Century). This reflects the railway experience which Nicholas Whittaker observed: *"In the fifties and sixties trainspotting was the Bash Street Kids versus British Rail... grumpy stationmasters and porters.... BUT ever since British Railways took up advertising jobs in the ABC spotting books, the railways have been staffed by former trainspotters. Not only do they get their chance to drive trains and whistle trains off, they welcome fellow enthusiasts with open arms."*

The BBC had realised that there was a commercial advantage in controlling the direction of the character. Again, the application of capitalist instincts reflects the railway experience. Nicholas Whittaker notes that by 1994, *"Privatization had already reared its ugly head... under the new rules locomotive owners must pay Railtrack for the privilege of travelling its rails. An extra cost that's too much for some of the preservation groups."*

The question in 2020 is not whether *Dr Who* has a future, but what direction that future might take. If there comes a time when the BBC can no longer support *Dr Who* as a TV show, will they "privatise it" and license it to a company like Netflix? Or will they hand it over to the preservationists?

I originally wrote "only time can tell" at this point, but was challenged by a correspondent*** who said that the question was irrelevant because the BBC *had* already attempted to privatise *Dr Who* with the TV movie. A good point, but I would argue the commercial environment was very different then. Despite the existence of of American *Dr Who* fan clubs watching old Jon Pertwee episodes on PBS, there was not a sizeable audience ready to embrace the McGann TV movie. Whereas now, a substantial worldwide audience has embraced the new-style *Dr Who*. So, could there come a time when the home grown BBC audience no longer justifies the BBC making the show – but the merchandising and worldwide audience make it attractive enough for the BBC to license the actual production of the series, so that the BBC can just sit back and benefit from the royalties?

*** Thanks Tomalak

La Grande Vadrouille or Don't Look Now – We're Being Shot At (1966)

In war time Paris, three RAF pilots are helped to escape the Nazi forces by the resistance. Sir Reginald (Terry-Thomas) is guided out into the countryside by decorator Augustin (Andre Bourvil) and orchestra conductor Stanlislas (Louis de Funes)

As the Buddhists say, the greatest treasures are always in the next field. La Grande Vadrouille (1966) translated as The Grand Tour – is the fifth most successful film in French cinema, France's equivalent of The Italian Job. A dubbed version was released in England by Rank in 1968 under the title Don't Look Now...We're Being Shot At! (on a double bill with Don Knotts as The Shakiest Gun In The West) and was screened on Scottish TV in 1995, but I'd never been aware of it. I only knew Andre Bourvil for his last role, the cynical Inspector Mattei in Le Cercle Rouge (1970), so it was a revelation to come across his more usual comic performance here.

I came across La Grande Vadrouille on an inflatable screen in July 2017 at an open air screening in St Helier on the island of Jersey. It had been organised as part of a Chamber of Commerce festival promoting Brittany. They'd set out 50 seats in the Weighbridge area, but ended up having to beg more chairs from the hotels. As the light fell (and the temperature dropped) an accordionist got the mood going playing period tunes such as Riccardo Del Turco's Luglio, (1968) which the French know as Le Petit Pain au chocolat and the British know as Herman's Hermits' Something is Happening (yes, of course I had to look that up).

As the summer sky stubbornly refused to give way to complete darkness, DJ Stefan Rousseau introduced the film to the English audience, explaining that Bourville and Louis de Funes were two of the most popular comic actors in France. There were plenty of French families in the audience and their reactions made it clear that this was a much-loved ritual movie – you could sense the "Don't tell him, Pike" or "Only supposed to blow the bloody doors off!" scenes as they started by the anticipation of the audience.

If it seemed odd watching a comedy about World War Two on an island that had been occupied by the Nazi's, it was worth remembering that the film was made by people who had lived through the occupation of France (for them the timescale had been the same as setting a 2020 movie in 1996). And as the movie ended to applause at 11pm, with Georges Auric's soaring theme carrying us into the night, it was certainly clear that this was a feel-good film.

Gerard Oury's movie has the same surreal overtones as other international spectacles such as Those Magnificent Men In Their Flying Machines . Terry-Thomas' bomber crew includes Peter, played by Mexican actor Claudio Brook (who had just starred in Bunuel's Simon of the Desert) while Canadian Alan is American actor Mike Marshall (who would later play space ranger Colonel Scott in Moonraker). When they jump from their blazing jet over Paris, Peter's parachute lands him on the scaffolding of decorator Augustin (Bourvil) while Alan lands on the roof of the Opera, where Stanislaus (de Funes) is trying to conduct a rehearsal. Squadron Leader Reginald (Terry-Thomas) parachutes into the seal pool of the Zoo.

The three have arranged to meet at the Turkish Baths in the Mosque and both Bourvile and De Funes separately agree to go in place of the British airmen. This gives rise to the first of a couple of surprisingly risque set-pieces as the naked Frenchmen cruise through the steamy bath, whistling the signal of Tea For Two, trying to identify which of the affronted men they come across is 'Big Moustache'.

As a contemporary review (or the pressbook puts it), "Bourvil and Louis de Funes are famous French comedians who are continually trying to get one up on each other. The comedy ranges from understatement to slapstick and farce, and is mainly visual. Each incident is built up so that the anticipation of the joke increases its effect." Louis de Funes has an energetic range of tics and reactions – in an early scene in his dressing room he puts the wig he's been wearing while conducting on a head block. When he stabs the wig with a knife to keep it secure he feels a jab in his head – and disbelievingly keeps stabbing the block, hurting himself more. Bourvil is more innocent – visually and in manner he comes across like a Yorkshireman – the contrast between the middle class and working man is underlined in an iconic scene where de Funes has to sit on Bourvil's shoulders because he's too short to climb over a wall.

Once he's over the wall, Bourvil asks him to get down, but with an elated smirk de Funes' says he's fine, rapping with his fist on Bourvil's helmet to get him to change direction.

The pursuing German forces include Hans Meyer (later to star in the Colditz TV series) and are led by the increasingly frustrated Benno Sterzenbach as Major Achbach. Sterzenbach does a fine slow burn as he tries to interrogate the babbling de Funes and Bourvil, but eventually leads his forces into Keystone Kops level slapstick. Oury pulls all the strands together with support from cinematographer Claude Renoir and composer Georges Auric (Passport to Pimlico, The Titfield Thunderbolt).

17 million Frenchmen can't be wrong – if you've not seen it La Grand Vadrouille is an undiscovered classic.

Project X

William Castle's Project X (1967) – out on Blu Ray from 101 Films – is like a fugitive from a frustrating dream where you go into the past and discover a book or comic that never really existed. If I'd ever heard of horror maestro William Castle directing a science fiction movie (1), it had never registered, so that enhances the feeling of coming across something from a parallel world!

The movie itself has the structure of a dream where the narrative suddenly shifts in strange unexpected ways. Christopher George (Grizzly, The Rat Patrol) plays 22nd Century geneticist Hagan Arnold who is sent on a secret spy mission to "Sino-Asia". He discovers a secret that will destroy America but his memory is wiped by an anti-interrogation drug injected before the mission by his own side. American scientists seek to recover his memory by an elaborate process which involves convincing him that he's a bank robber in 1960's America.

When I read the precis on the back of the Blu Ray, I assumed this would be a cheap way filming a lot of the movie on 1960's city streets. But surprisingly this action takes place in a reproduction of a remote farmhouse flung together by the 22nd Century military. It's almost like Mission: Impossible with the main cast of scientists assuming false identities. The casting of actors like Philip Pine and Henry Jones who regularly guest-starred in 1960's TV shows and Van Cleave's spot-on jazzy score during this sequence heightens the resemblance to a Quinn Martin production. *

*Christopher George himself would later star in the Quinn Martin TV movie The House on Greenapple Road (1970). The subsequent series, Dan August saw Burt Reynolds take the lead – George was already starring in The Immortal (1970-71).

When the amnesiac George sleeps, scientist Henry Jones uses a mind-scanning process to creates holograms reproducing what is known of George's mission in the hope that his sub-conscious will then reveal what is unknown. This leads to the most incredible development of the whole film. It's almost as if William Castle actually journeyed forward into the 21st Century and saw a modern day thriller with all the computer generated stunts and special effects! And on returning to the 1960's, he did his best to recreate what he'd seen by commissioning Hanna Barbera to animate the dream sequences. George and other actors are superimposed over cartoon sequences designed by Carl Urbano and Alex Toth (at least some of which are retreads from the Jonny Quest TV show).

Scriptwriter Edmund Morris (another TV veteran) effectively reverses the plot of Leslie P. Davies' novel The Artificial Man (1965). In the book, the hero is a science fiction writer living in a 1960's village. Friends and neighbours keep making remarks which inspire the development of a novel he is writing about life in a dictatorship in 2016. After he meets a girl from the village who believes she is living in 2016, the author gradually realises that he's a secret agent who has lost his memory. It really is 2016 and his life as a writer has been part of a plot to recover the secrets held in his lost memory. There are obvious overtones of the 1967 TV series The Prisoner and it's intriguing that Castle and North chose to give the big revelation right at the start of the movie – as if they wanted to make sure they didn't confuse anyone.

We only get vague hints of what the world of the future is like – women are designated as sterile or breeders, and nobody knows what a potato is. There's an implication of the dictatorship of Davies' novel, but since most of the action takes place in a top secret military project it's hard to be certain. Harold Gould plays the Colonel in charge of the operation, constantly in opposition to Jones and Pine as the scientists. There's a slight hint of Waiting for Godot watching actors who usually play supporting roles taking the lead – you're constantly waiting for the big star to turn up – but with even George laying comatose or addled for much of the movie, it's Jones and Gould who dominate. There's a darkly amusing scene at one point when it's feared that the project has been exposed to a plague – and Jones calmly lays out to a horrified Gould how they'll have to quarantine the base as the infection spreads , with each new victim cremated by the survivors. Jones delivers this speech with a methodical slyness, so we're never quite sure if he's already thought of the loophole that's going to save them.

The second source for the movie is Davies' novel The Psychogeist, which has similar themes of amnesia, a man recalling a childhood comic which may actually be memories of life on an alien planet, and a top secret project. When scientist Jones comments during one scene that, "What we see in the mirror and what the mind sees filtered through our ego is quite another thing." he seems to be stating the main theme of Davies' work.

It's possible that The Psychogeist inspired the character of Gregory Gallea, the mysterious figure played by Monte Markham (star of The Second Hundred Years TV series – later to be the Seven Million Dollar Man rival of The Six Million Dollar Man). Markham wears an Ed Bishop catsuit and a Roger Delgado beard so he looks like a futuristic villain, but plays Gallea with a convincing ambiguity, so we're never quite sure of his connection with George and the mysterious disembodied entity that manifests itself in the project (2). Picking up a plot strand from The Artificial Man, George's character has met a girl from the village (Greta Baldwin) who is unaware of the deception. When she's arrested by the military, Markham tries to enlist her aid in busting George out of the project. Once again, just when you think you know what direction the movie's going in, Castle veers off in another direction.

As a piece of science fiction, Project X often looks outdated, and as a work made for hire it looks cheap – especially in comparison to some of the other movies coming out at the time. But it has a kind of mad charm and beneath the surface there are a number of interesting concepts, not just as science fiction but in relation to other films (3)

(1) In fact, Spine Tingler: The William Castle Story (2007) on the Indicator 13 Ghosts Blu Ray, does mention Project X as a project handed to Castle by the studio before Rosemary's Baby but released as an anti-climactic follow-up to the success of the Ira Levin adaptation.

The 101 Films Blu Ray of Project X comes with a commentary by Allan Bryce and David Flint and a new documentary, Money Back Guarantee in which commentators such as Vic Pratt (above) of the BFI relate William Castle's career in ballyhoo. It's obviously cut price in comparison to the documentaries on the recent Indicator box set, but then cut price is well in the spirit of Castle and Project X – and it still manages to be entertaining and informative.

(2) SPOILER – Gallea is the villain, albeit one with a convincing motivation. One could only wish the next actor to play The Master on Doctor Who could be given a Ludovico Treatment and sat in front of Markham's performance as Gallea so they can see there is another way to play a villain without going full Jack Nicholson/Johnny Depp.

(3) SPOILER *** The movie ends with Henry Jones telling Greta Baldwin that George has been given a new identity and new memories as an engineer. Baldwin is informed that she also has a new identity and that she was officially married to George three days ago. George affects a particular vacuousness in his new identity and as they depart hand-in-hand it's hard to dispel memories of Arnold Shwarzenegger and Sharon Stone in Total Recall.

12

Til Death Us Do Part (1968)

Till Death us do Part is that rarity – a movie spun-off from a TV show which feels like it adds more to the story. Director Norman Cohen, who would go on to helm the first film version of Dad's Army (1971) also directed the semi-documentary The London Nobody Knows (1969 – based on Geoffrey Fletcher's book) which may explain the authenticity of this movie.

Johnny Speight's 1966 BBC TV series was contemporary – so contemporary that sometimes the scripts were late – and usually centred upon arguments between Alf Garnett (Warren Mitchell), his son-in-law Mike (Anthony Booth) and daughter Rita (Una Stubbs), both of whom lodged with Alf and wife Else (Dandy Nichols) in their terraced house in Wapping.

The movie was made by British Lion soon after the TV series had been cancelled in mid-1968. The lateness of Speight's scripts is given as one reason for the cancellation, although the controversy over the political arguments in the show (and Garnett's frequent use of the then-offensive word bloody) made the show unpopular with an incoming BBC management. Speight and Cohen give the movie an epic scope by devoting the first hour to the Second World War.

Opening with a black-and-white newsreel showing Nazi tanks massing, the movie picks up Alf Garnett's commentary, *"They're all cardboard! He's probably got men inside pedalling! It's all propaganda! That's yer Goebbels- he's famous for it! Propaganda!"*

Throughout the TV series there had been controversy over whether Speight was satirising or espousing Garnett's bigoted views, but with a wartime setting it is clear that Garnett is the archetypal pub bore. An early scene shows drinkers listening in silence as Garnett puts forward his theory that Dunkirk is actually part of Churchill's grand strategy to strengthen the British forces. And before that, Garnett is shown being taken by surprise in his tin bath, when Chamberlain announces that the war Alf said would never happen, is actually happening.

After the first hour the action jumps forward the March 1966 General Election and Alf arguing with daughter Rita (Una Stubbs) about whether she can put a Labour poster in his window. Cohen captures the frenetic world of the TV series well – Una Stubbs' affection and exasperation coming across as she argues with Alf while clearing the plates from the table (Dandy Nichols, sitting at the table as Else, neutral in the argument, suddenly puts her hand on Una's to stop her taking the Swiss Roll away). Terry Knight's detailed set design captures the mood of the 1960's – halfway between Victorian and Elizabethan ages – Una's micro mini skirt and mod design washing up liquid set against the 1930's kitchen implements and wallpaper.

Garnett's home (ironically shown as Jamaica Street by an insert when Alf mistakenly receives call-up papers) is represented by a lovingly created external set at Shepperton, which allows Cohen to take the characters through the 'phony war', the blitz, VE day, and through to the 1960's. Powerfully, this also allows Speight to represent the experience of actual Londoners. Having survived the bombs, the Garnett's find that their house is listed for demolition by the council (the actual Garnet Street in Wapping had already been demolished). When valuers arrive to put through the compulsory purchase, Alf is told that his house is worth £400.

"But I bought it off the Council for Fifteen Hundred," Alf protests, "And they gave me a mortgage!" The valuer (Frank Thornton) explains that £400 is the land value. There is no property value.

Alf refuses to sell, but the bulldozers move in, his local pub is boarded up and workmen begin to gut the neighbouring houses. Finally, Alf arrives home to find Else, Mike and Rita packing up and moving to the new tower block, where the council offer luxuries such as an indoor toilet. Defeated, Alf finally follows . But as he arrives at the brutalist concrete block, he realises he doesn't know the apartment number. He begins knocking on doors as, on a lower level, the family go out to the cinema.

When the TV series returned in 1970, the climax of the movie was ignored and the Garnett's were still settled in their terraced house*.

*In the TV episode, 'Dock Pilfering' (11 October 1972) Alf is gloating that the house is now worth £20,000 under a Tory Government, whereas it was only worth £600 under Labour. When Mike counters that it is just inflation, Alf retorts that, "According to Labour" the £2.00 a week Mike pays in rent is now worth only 25 shillings (£1.25). So, "On the black day you married my daughter and moved in here you were paying £2.00 a week rent in a £600 house. But, now thanks to me and the Tory Government, you're only paying 25 shillings rent for a room in a £20,000 house! Under us, YOU'VE GOT ON!"

Set against the context of the TV series, the end of the movie may be disconcerting, but it's a small price to pay. The film itself hangs together well. Perhaps because the movie had to pass the British Board of Film censors, there are only few of Garnett's more outrageous racial comments and most of those are filtered through the wartime sequences (one slightly ugly scene with actress Cleo Sylvestre is singled out for inclusion in the original trailer, suggesting that the producers were trying to capitalise on the controversy of the TV shows).

However, the movie is generally funny, if you can be entertained by seeing man at his most craven and self-interested. The scene where Alf, craving some milk for his tea at a time of wartime rationing, snatches baby Rita's milk bottle and tries to unobtrusively lighten his tea before Else comes back in the room has echoes of Laurel and Hardy .

50 Years of James Burke (7 July 2019)

The future is just a past that hasn't happened yet. And the past is all too dependent on our memories. Nothing proves this more than the 6 July 2019 issue of **Radio Times** , which carries two articles by James Burke in his inimitable* style. The first recalls the excitement of the Moonshot in July 1969. The second is a reprint of the 1969 **Radio Times** in which Burke looks forward to covering the Moonshot.

(*and yes, I proved it is inimitable by trying to imitate it there)

Burke puts the Moon Landing in context for those who weren't born then (and those of us who have forgotten). *"In 1969, Britain had towns full of smoke-blackened buildings, half the population had no TV or cars – or inside loos. We all lived with the awareness (buried deep in our brains) that any day might bring a nuclear attack."* More to the point, he makes it clear that the Moon Shot and its TV coverage didn't go according to plan!Check out the reprint from 1969, and you'll see James Burke from 50 years ago telling us that after touchdown, Armstrong and Aldrin would spend two hours checking the systems before swallowing sleeping pills. "Four hours later they wake, eat and at just after seven-twelve am on Monday July 21, Neil Armstrong goes down the ladder."

With the benefit of hindsight, 2019 James Burke tells us it didn't go that way. *"I heard them doing stuff that indicated a change of plan (preparing their moon-walk suits and not rigging sleep hammocks), so it was time for a re-think and the first-ever BBC all-night TV. "One small step" happened for a UK audience of 22 million at 3.56 am."*

Those of us too young to stay up woke the next day to Neil Armstrong's descent being played on a loop. There was a small sense of being cheated – why hadn't they had the courtesy to wait for British breakfast time?

But the two articles by Burke remind us that just because something's written down, it doesn't mean it happened that way. The whole Moon Shot was planned to the second. But there was always a *chance* that something could change.

22 years later, James Burke brought out a book called **Chances** and I found that pretty life changing.

It's basically a book of facts. Or a book of odds. Posed as questions about everyday life. Which dogs are more likely to bite? (*Alsatians, Chow, Airedale and Pekinese)* What are the chances I will die before my 25-year mortgage is paid off? (*For a 30 year old male, 1 in 9).* The blurb on the back tells us that, *"Since 1981 AIDS has killed 500,000 people. In the same period 16,000,000 have died from measles… If you are likely to be shot, poisoned or strangled it will probably happen in*

December and there's a 64 per cent chance you will know your murderer... but don't worry... you are 14 times more likely to have killed yourself first!"

There is no index or bibliography, although there is an acknowledgement "to Helen O'Leary for her meticulous research." But then it's not that kind of book. It was published by Virgin Publishing (remember them?) and sold for £2.99. That sounds like a pittance now – it's the equivalent of £6.30 today. I doubt you could buy a new paperback for that price today although that might be because a modern publisher would make the book bigger – with a larger, more spaced-out typeface – to push the page count and retail price up. Holding **Chances** you remember that paperbacks were once – like mobile phones – a piece of entertainment you could carry in your pocket.

So why do I call **Chances** life changing? James Burke says at the start that, *"Life is a gamble....Forecasting the future is a matter of knowing the influences that determine the outcome (of your decisions)."*

Flicking through the book in the WH Smiths on Paddington station back in 1992, I came across the following line: "Are trustful people more likely to enjoy good mental/emotional health than the mistrustful?" And the answer was: *"Yes. A variety of studies show that trustful people, far from being the gullible, naïve types who are victimised by others, are actually... far better liked and have far fewer mental/emotional problems."*

And next to it was the question, "Are people who mistrust others more likely to be untrustworthy themselves?" And the answer was: *"Yes. According to a number of studies, people who tend to be suspicious of others are themselves more likely to be cheats, manipulators and liars."*

As I said, £2.99 seemed like a lot of money back then, so I didn't buy the book, although I certainly took the thought away with me.

I was a pretty negative person at the time – and while this wasn't a 'Road to Damascus' it did start me thinking that there was a possibility the glass might be half full instead of half empty. Or that there might be some benefit in presuming that the glass was half full. So as much as anything could be deemed "life changing" this book was it. So thank you, James Burke. Long may you write.

That Old Black Magic

That Old Black Magic (2018) by Cathi Unsworth. This is not going to be a long review. I was completely beguiled by this book. I got into it very easily and had to ration the chapters after I got half way through because I didn't want it to end too soon.

It's set in 1940's Britain and follows Detective Sergeant Ross Spooner as he hunts a German agent in wartime Birmingham. At the heart of the story is the mystery of a murdered woman whose remains were found inside an old wych elm tree in 1943. Although she was never identified, mysterious graffitti began to appear a year later asking, "Who put Bella in the wych elm?" Spooner also encounters Helen Duncan, a real-life medium and the last person to be tried for witchcraft in Britain after she revealed the secret news of the sinking of HMS Barham at a seance.

This isn't one of those Harry Potter of Scotland Yard thrillers that are popular now. It's solidly grounded in the real world, with a lurking question of whether the supernatural really exists. MI5 gives Spooner a cover as a theatrical agent and this gives him an excuse to roam the pubs and theatres of blackout Britain. Cathi Unsworth conjures a convincing sense of time and place. It wasn't until page 293 that I came across something I questioned as anachronistic. I actually wrote it down because it made me realise how completely I'd been taken in until that point.*

Unsworth says in the acknowledgements that she felt Dennis Wheatley had been an "avuncular spirit guide" – a comment that brought me up sharp because a couple of times, I had thought That Old Black Magic was like a Dennis Wheatley thriller without the patrician lectures. That does create a dilemma. The question everybody asks about crime thrillers is, "are there any plans to turn it into a movie?" But really, it would take Terence Fisher and the Hammer Films of The Devil Rides Out (1968) to do That Old Black Magic justice.

*It was the use of the term "gig", which research now tells me was first documented in Melody Maker in 1926 and therefore could have been used in the 1940's. It was the curse of 21st Century neoliberalism that threw me. But it also indicates how convincing the book is in general .

That Old Black Magic by Cathi Unsworth. Serpent's Tail/Profile Books £12.99 ISBN 978 1 78125 727 2

Cairo Road (1950)

Cairo Road is a police procedural, filmed partly on location in Egypt. Eric Portman stars as implacable Colonel Youssef Bey, leading Laurence Harvey's headstrong Lt Mourad, in a mission to disrupt a gang smuggling drugs down the "Poison Road" into Cairo.

Inspired by made-on-location thrillers like T Men (1947) and Naked City (1948), producer Aubrey Baring of Mayflower pictures insisted on director David MacDonald's crew spending seven weeks filming establishing shots in Cairo's streets, docks and markets. The screenplay by Robert Westerby (Cone of Silence (1960) and The Scarecrow of Romney Marsh (1963)) was written with the co-operation of the Egyptian government, which gave access to the case files of its Anti-Narcotics Bureau. Made at a time when there were estimated to be only 50 (mostly wealthy) heroin addicts in Britain, the film painted a picture of a country already blighted by the illegal drugs trade.

Cairo Road opens with Lt Mourad being called to a murder scene in Cairo's old market, after drugs are found in the victim's pockets. 22-year-old Laurence Harvey showed an improvement over his stiff movie debut as the villain in House of Darkness (1949). According to Cairo Road's publicity, "Larry has been carefully groomed by Associated British to whom he is under contract (and) shows he has a big future." Mourad theorises that the victim was stabbed by someone expecting to find a large shipment of drugs, but the shipment was delayed. Colonel Youssef Bey (Eric Portman) is unimpressed by the "rather bumptious" Mourad until his investigation links the victim Bashiri to the Pavlis brothers. Colonel Bey (Eric Portman) had jailed drugs distributor Eduardo Pavlis (Czech actor Karl Stepanek), but smuggler Rico remains at large importing heroin slabs "trademarked" with a portrait of Youssef Bey. Eduardo Pavlis, nearing the end of his three year sentence at Tura Farm Prison, idolises his brother. He reacts to a remark by Youssef Bey about Rico Pavlis skulking around importing drugs, shouting: "When you are all so stupid there is no need for him to skulk. He comes, he goes. You couldn't know him. You've never seen him! "

Spoiler: The Following Paragraph Reveals an Important Plot Development which could impair your enjoyment of the film.

Publicity for Cairo Road advised that "Harold Lang, another screen newcomer, proves himself a chiller-specialist in the role of Cairo's No 1 dope smuggler." When we first see Lang, he is on board a passenger ship in the guise of a British engine salesman called Humble. He is trying to make conversation with Anna Michelis (Egyptian star Camelia) who the audience knows is a courier carrying heroin into Egypt. With a delivery slightly reminiscent of entertainer Des O'Connor, Humble cheerfully tells her that "I've been snubbed by three men and frozen out by you."

Humble has seen her in conversation with Lombardi (Gregoire 'Coco' Aslan) and quizzes her relationship with him. Anna says Lombardi was just trying to pick her up

18

and returns to her cabin, telling Humble he's boring her. Sauntering near the radio cabin Humble overhears a Morse Code message indicating that the police want the crew to detain Anna. When he quizzes the ship's officer (Peter Jones) he's told to stay out of it and keep his mouth shut. But Humble spots Lombardi on deck and questions whether he also understands Morse code. Later that night, Anna is subjected to a murderous attack.

It's only revealed halfway through the movie that Humble is actually Rico Pavlis. By then he's convinced both us and the police of his identity (the screenplay continues to refer to him as Humble). Both Harvey and Portman are rather austere characters and Humble has been more of an audience identification character up to this point. Lang adopts a cold-eyed, abrupt delivery as Rico, although retaining his British accent. His movements are economic, even when furiously advancing on an informer to garrotte him. In a later scene, Lang is striding through a Suez street trying to evade a police dragnet when Laurence Harvey calls out to him. Lang, as Pavlis, puts a hand to the gun beneath his jacket, approaching the Lieutenant with a cold, calculating manner. Then, as Harvey continues to chatter, Lang withdraws his hand and his expression softens into the matey features of Humble as he conjures up a story to take advantage of the young policeman.

As in other police procedurals, the young officer is used to introduce the audience to the methods of the single-minded Youssef Bey who trusts no-one. Bey leads his men to disrupt the three routes used by the Pavlis gang to bring their drugs into Egypt. It's a strange mix of ancient and modern, with camels being led through a scanner at the border post to detect swallowed drugs, and Bedouin tribesmen being chased down by the "Camel Corps" as they try to make an escape.

Although the film was made with the support of the Egyptian Government, which gave permission to film in Tura Farm Prison and Abassia Mental Hospital, the film had censorship problems within the UK. The subject matter made it difficult to achieve the more profitable general admission A certificate (the new X category had just been introduced to exclude children under 16).

In the early stages of the film Mourad doubts the seriousness of the drug threat. Youssef Bey takes him to see Farghani (Thomas Gallagher), who was arrested with Eduardo Pavlis but later moved to the Mental Hospital. John Bailey (later Edward Waterfield, in the Doctor Who story Evil of the Daleks) plays the unnamed doctor at the asylum. The original script directions say that, "the compounds hold many men who are people no longer. Some sit motionless in the dust, some sing gently to themselves. Other beg for cigarettes, tonelessly like men talking in their sleep." In the film, we only see Bailey leading Harvey to the door of a barred ward. "These patients are here because they were destroyed by opium. They're alive. But dead. Some of them were poor and stupid. Some of them were good men. But the drug is a great leveller. Now they're all the same. All nothing." The doctor lets him into a barred ward and shuts the door behind him saying. "Look". It's reminiscent of the scene in

The Third Man where Holly Martins is forced to view the children maimed by Harry Lime's black market penicillin. Mourani is similarly shocked by what he sees.

Colonel Youssef Bey insists on seeing Farghani, a former doctor who aided the Pavlis gang. The mental home doctor says Farghani was "..was a doctor. A good doctor. A friend of mine. He worked too hard and started living on his nerves. At the hospital he had access to drugs. And he stole them. That was at the top of the slide." putting him under the control of the Pavlis gang. The doctor says Farghani has mentally retreated, "He tells himself he is somewhere else." Unimpressed, Portman insists on interrogating Farghani (Thomas Gallagher). The script notes that, "The man stares dully in front of him. His hands are restless all the time. , but otherwise he is very still. (and) to satisfy Censors requirements, Farghani's face is never seen."

It appears that the censors wished to emphasise the moral risk of drugs, but thought showing the effects of addiction would be too much for viewers under 16.

Last minute revisions, also seem to have caused the ending to be reshot. The shooting script resolves the early conflict between the two stars. Mourad makes his final report to Youssef Bey and is about to go home with his wife (French actress Maria Mauban). As they leave the phone rings with news of another incident. Bey says he will attend, and Mourad standing in the doorway, exchanges a look of agreement with his wife before saying he will come along. "It never ends, does it?"

In the movie, a stand-in dressed as Mourad stands in front of Beys desk. Portman sums up the case and then tells Mourad to go home to his wife. As the stand-in leaves, Portman answers the phone, agreeing to attend the latest incident and then uttering the closing words, "It never ends." Whether the censor objected to the scripted ending because it suggested a personal cost to law enforcers relationships, or perhaps not all the actors were available, it follows close on the curiously truncated climax to leave viewers with the feeling that something is missing.

However, last-minute rewrites can't be blamed for a final mystery. It ranks with the riddle of "Who Shot the Chauffer" in The Big Sleep. The final showdown is a tense affair but it rests on both Pavlis brothers being unaware that their agent Bashiri is dead. The newly released Eduardo is effusive, clearly idolising his brother, while Rico is more edgy, trying to downplay the mayhem he's caused. But both think the arrival of Bashiri will allow them to recover their losses.

Rico has earlier confirmed (to Anna's controller and the audience) that "Anna was just a name to me" and that he killed her to protect himself. But Rico also tells her controller that Bashiri is someone he can trust. So who killed Bashiri? Was it another gang, trying to move in on the Pavlis brothers trade? Was there a sub-plot that fell by the wayside? We may never know.

Harold Lang

"The most fascinating and perhaps the cleverest man I have ever known." John Fraser

"A great, slightly manic actor." Alan Plater

Harold Lang played Christie, the private detective who slips Richard Wordsworth out of hospital in 'The Quatermass Experiment' (1955). Christie makes the fatal mistake of demanding to see what he's got hidden up his sleeve.

He was the night club owner who organises Roy Castle's fateful Caribbean gig in "Dr Terror's House of Horrors" (1965). In Hammer's Paranoic (1963) he was a satirical bar-fly whose attempt at peace-making earns the threat of a handful of darts from a soused Oliver Reed. In The Psychopath (1966) he was the wistful toy salesman who bemoans modern children's fondness for war toys.

Harold Lang was also a passionate advocate of Constantin Stanislavski's acting "method", a performer who toured the world demonstrating Shakespearian techniques and a teacher whose acting classes were captured in a film by John Schlesinger. Lang appeared with Patrick Wymark in several pivotal plays and films. On the stage, he directed one of Olwen Wymark's early plays and tragically Patrick Wymark's last. Olwen Wymark's 1971 collection, 'The Gymnasium and Other Plays' is dedicated, "to Patrick and to Harold."

In his 2004 book Close Up John Fraser describes Lang as having, " a shock of white-blonde hair, a cruel slash of a mouth with no lips at all, and a brisk, small-stepping gait which was 'camp' without being effeminate at all…His devoted admirers included Kenneth Tynan, Robert Shaw, Margaret Drabble… Alec Guinness and many others…"

Harold Lang was born 1923 in London. He studied acting at RADA where, despite rebelling against the classical curriculum he took the 1942 Bancroft Gold Medal for best actor. His first stage role was with the Midland Theatre Company before joining the Young Vic to play at the Arts Theatre. Lang first attracted attention in 1955 playing Edmund in a Shakespeare Memorial theatre production King Lear opposite John Gielgud. He later toured Europe with the company.

His first credited film role was in as a pickpocket in The Spider & the Fly (1949) written by Robert Westerby and directed by Robert Hamer as his follow-up to Kind Hearts and Coronets (also 1949). Lang has only a few lines in two short scenes with the film's star Eric Portman. The first, in which Portman's French detective compels him to reverse a theft displays the authoritative movement by which Lang could expand the scripted role. The second, in which Lang informs on Guy Rolfe's aristocratic cat burglar, displays his economic underlining of character in the lines. He had already developed the very subtle mid-Atlantic delivery that he employed in many performances. For a long time I was puzzled because his accent reminded me of someone - and it was only with the death of variety artist Des O'Connor that I realised Harold Lang reminded me of O'Connor.

The following year, he was fourth down the cast list in Westerby's filmed-on-location thriller Cairo Road. Over the next few years, Lang played character roles in a number of films including Wendy Toye's The Franchise Affair ((1951), and Terence Fisher's Wings of Danger(1952).

In 1953 he played a member of Terence Morgan's gang in Muriel Box's semi-documentary Street Corner, starring Barbara Murray as a Woman Police Officer. Lang appears in three scenes, first setting up a robbery, later doing a bit of scene-stealing in a night club, his lips moving as he reads a newspaper while Morgan and Michael Medwin discuss the plot. Lang's final scene is when Morgan is on the run with Peggy Cummins and hides out at Lang's flat. Cummins starts rooting through the kitchen for food and an affronted Lang sneers, "I usually eat out."

In the same year, Lang was employed again by Robert Hamer for his film noir, The Long Memory . Lang has the small role of assistant to the movie's sneering villain Boyd (John Chandos) who has framed John Mills for manslaughter. We first see Lang as the unhelpful receptionist of Boyd's office at Shad Thames, fending off queries from both Elizabeth Sellars and the police, but he later dons a cap to act as Boyd's chauffeur. For most of the film Lang takes a subordinate role, but when Chandos chases John Mills towards the end and lets off a shot at him, Lang suddenly grabs the pistol with a quiet reprimand of, "naughty". Lang's cocky assurance when the police interrogate him later, gives the impression that he's part of a larger organisation - a criminal civil servant who will continue working, whatever happens to his "minister" (Boyd).

Lang continued to act in films throughout the 1950's, including Murder By Proxy (1954), Men of Sherwood Forest(1954) and Chain of Events (1958). During the same period he continued to appear on stage. In February 1955, for instance, he played the dissolute Camille Raquin in The Lovers, an adaptation of Emile Zola's novel Therese Raquin.. The play starred Eva Bartok (Blood and Black Lace) as Therese, and director Sam Wanamaker as her lover Laurent. Lang attracted praise for his "clever performance" as the victim of the murder plot.

In the same period Lang established a growing reputation as a commentator. In July 1956 he criticised and discussed the Observer Film Exhibition (celebating sixty years of cinema) with organiser Richard Buckle on the Home Service (Radio 4). He also tackled a diverse range of stage roles.

22

In the same year he teamed up with critic Kenneth Tynan to write The Quest for Corbett, a radio play performed on the Third Programme (Radio 3), in July of 1956. Billed as a satirical parody of the biographical radio feature, it starred actress and writer Naomi Jacob as authoress and adventurer Aphra Corbett. In 1958 Harold Lang played one of his favourite roles as Sam Levy, the dying, and later dead father of John Fraser in Bernard Kops' The Hamlet of Stepney Green , first at the Oxford Theatre and later at the Lyric, Hammersmith.

In 1959 Casper Wrede established the 59 Theatre Company for a six month season at the Lyric Theatre, Hammersmith with Michael Elliott as assistant artistic director. One of their first productions was Danton's Death in which Lang played Robespierre, opposite Patrick Wymark in the title role. This was followed by "The Cheats of Scapin", a farce by Thomas Otway adapted from Moliere. Lang starred as Scapin, the deceitful servant of Gripe (Patrick Wymark). Scapin schemes to help two young lovers stay together against the desires of their parents. As well as his stage success, Lang also became a familiar face on TV. In 1961 he appeared as DaRica in several episodes of John Bowen and Jeremy Bulmore's 'Garry Halliday' (BBC1's predecessor of Dr Who). On 8th October 1961 he appeared on ABC's Armchair Theatre in Alun Owen's "The Rose Affair" while on 27 October 1961 he played a doss house resident who forges a job reference for a young man in "The Referees" the first TV play by Alan Plater. In October 1962, he starred with Jon Pertwee and Moira Lister in See You Inside, a revue written by Barry Cryer with songs by Ted Dicks. Significantly, Lang's role as compere included a witty discussion about what stage revue's should be and what this particular revue was attempting. Unfortunately, a sketch about President Kennedy had to be cut on the orders of the Lord Chamberlain (who still licensed and censored stage plays until 1968) because reference to a Head of State could not be allowed. Highest praise came for a sketch in which Moira Lister tries to launch a ship with a champagne bottle that keeps bouncing back to her hand.

Lang's career suggests an eclectic, energetic individual, eager to popularise the classics but always open to new experiences. In 1960 he directed T.S. Eliot's The Cocktail Party for a tour of India, Pakistan and Sri Lanka by the Oxford Theatre Company. On his return he spoke on the Radio 3 programme 'Talking of Theatre' about how he went to teach western technique but became an admirer of Indian theatre. A devotee of Stanislavski's acting "method" (emphasising movement, observation and motivation) he was invited to join the staff of the Central School of Speech and Drama. He made his acceptance conditional on the school also hiring Yat Malmgren, the Swedish teacher of character through movement who is credited with having coached Sean Connery.

While students were able to choose most of the elements of their own curriculum, Lang's acting class was compulsory. In April 1962 John Schlesinger filmed 'The Class', "a tribute to Lang's riveting teaching method," for the BBC1 series Monitor, showing him training a first year class. Lang also appeared in "A Film Profile" of Elia Kazan, film director and co-founder of the "Actors Studio" on BBC1 on 25 April 1962. In 1963, Lang gave a striking demonstration of character through movement when he portrayed Silent, the police informer in Michael Winner's "West 11" ("I'm like you," Lang tells Alfred Lynch, tapping his forehead, "I've got it up here.")

In that same year, Lang and seven other teachers left the Central School of Drama in protest at the sacking of Yat Malmgren. Lang would later be invited to teach at the Drama Centre, London, co-founded by Malmgren. But before that Lang consolidated his theories about acting, collaborating with Nicholas Amer, and Greville Hallam in Macbeth in Camera , a "Didactic Comedy" about the techniques an actor needs to bring Shakespeare's printed text to life. Together with David Kelsey they formed the Voyage Theatre Company to tour Australia, New Zealand and South America under the auspices of the British Council (Macbeth in Camera was filmed by Australia's ABC TV and was still being screened in November 1975).

Macbeth in Camera took place in a rehearsal room during a village arts festival. David Kelsey as uptight academic organiser Geoffrey Kerr Ph.D. confronted a couple of actors (Amer and Hallam) rehearsing Macbeth. Kerr threatened to eject them from the festival because of director Harold Lang's approach, breaking the Shakespearean dialogue into everyday speech in order to explore the underlying meaning. During the course of the two hour play, the actors attempted to convince the academic that their approach could expose the reality behind the action. Frequent passages from the play were enlivened by the argument about the need to understand the meaning behind Shakespeare's words. Critics praised the naturalism of the actors, which convinced the audience they were seeing something spontaneous. Critics noted Harold Lang's expressive gestures and he was praised by one reviewer as, "One of the most natural actors I've ever watched." At the end of the first half, Lang turned to the audience and murmured, "We're going for a cup of coffee." , wandering off with the others, without dropping a curtain.

In 1964, Lang wrote Man Speaking using the works of Milton, Blake and John Donne to explore British poetry. Together with Amer and Hallam, Lang discussed the interpretation and performance of verse, taking poetry down off its pedestal and subjecting it to scrutiny. In November 1965 Lang spoke about the aims of the Voyage Theatre Company on the Home Service radio show "The Lively Arts". For the next two years, under the sponsorship of the British Council, the company toured with Macbeth in Camera , Man Speaking and A Sleep of Prisoners by Christopher Fry. In June 1966, Lang used recordings from the shows to illustrate a Home Service discussion called "What Makes An Actor" before the company appeared in the Philippines where the promotor dubbed the Voyage Theatre, "The Intellectual

Beatles". Harold Lang later lived up to this billing when he performed poetry as a guest of folk singer Julie Felix on the 24 Feb 1968 episode of her BBC 2 series "Once More With Felix".

1968 was a busy TV year for Lang. On 24 January 1968, he appeared in Jean Anouilh's BBC1 Wednesday Play, Monsieur Barnet, playing off Miriam Karlin as a sinister hairdresser/manicurist combination discussing the sexual appetites of their customer Sir Michael Redgrave. On 3 February he played Nat, the camp and conniving proprietor of 'Anatole's Hairdressing Salon' in the Public Eye episode Memories of Meg (TV World ran an article on Lang to promote this episode). In March 1968, Lang co-starred with Patrick Wymark in the Playhouse adaptation of " The Detour., playing a railway engineer whose wife convinces him to help her get revenge on a former lover. And in April 1968, he appeared as the Chief Eunuch in an episode of the Victorian spoof, Virgin of the Secret Service.

By June 1969, Harold Lang was referred to as "one of the most respected men in British theatre" when he directed one of Olwen Wymark's first plays "The Technicians" at the Phoenix Theatre, Leicester. Part of a double bill called "By-Play" with "The Straight Man", Wymark's play was an attack on artificiality in British theatre. Lang also starred as one of the alien "technicians" who take over the personalities of a bickering married couple.

In early 1970, Lang made a four month tour of Uganda, Tanzania, Mauritius and Kenya. On his return, he agreed to direct Patrick Wymark and John Fraser in the Australian production of Sleuth . The play opened successfully in Sydney, but Patrick Wymark passed away during the run on 20 October 1970. Sadly, Harold Lang also had a heart attack while travelling home through Egypt and died on 16 November 1970 in a Cairo hospital aged forty-seven.

At the time of his death, Harold Lang was making preparations for the March 1971 premiere at Sadlers Wells of Elisabeth Luytens opera, Time Off? Not a Ghost of a Chance . Lang had collaborated on the libretto with Luytens (who scored The Psychopath and Dr Terror's House of Horrors) and was to have played a leading role.

As a result of Lang's death, the New Opera Company cancelled the production. The opera eventually premiered at Sadlers Wells in April 1973 as part of a live broadcast on Radio 3. Lang had also sold a script to London Weekend Television, and Just In Time For Christmas the tale of University Professor Nottage (Alfred Burke) whose wife Janet (Gwen Watford) announces after 20 years of marriage that she is pregnant, was broadcast on December 23rd 1972.

A restless and energetic individual, Harold Lang left a diverse body of work behind him, but doubtless the best was yet to come.

Captured

Four years before joining 'The Plane Makers', Alan Dobie starred in CAPTURED, a 64 minute film training film with the impact of a full scale movie. Written and directed by John Krish, who would later make UNEARTHLY STRANGER and THE MAN WHO HAD POWER OVER WOMEN, the film was commissioned by the British Army to teach servicemen how to resist brainwashing techniques experienced in Korea. Although Krish had hoped the film would serve as a show reel to help him break into feature films, CAPTURED was classified as restricted and was not to be seen outside military installations until 2004.

While Krish's misunderstanding may seem naive in retrospect, it's worth remembering that the concept of brainwashing was hardly a military secret. It had been the subject of several Hollywood movies such as THE RACK (1956) in which Paul Newman is put on trial for collaborating while a Prisoner Of War in Korea, and THE FEARMAKERS (1958). However, CAPTURED was intended as a training film, looking not back at the past but forward to the future.

CAPTURED has an impressive cast. Bernard Fox, the Welsh actor who specialised in 'fake Englishmen' (Colonel Crittenden in Hogans Heroes, Dr Bombay in Bewitched, Captain Havlock in THE MUMMY) has a low-key role as the officer briefing Dobie's intelligence corporal and a sergeant (played by Gerald Flood from 'The Rat Catchers') who is about to go out on a scouting mission. When Dobie is caught, he meets up with Wilfrid Bramble (pre 'Steptoe and Son') as a bolshy old soldier who spent several years in a German Prisoner of War camp. Dobie warns him that things could be different in Korea.

The film is introduced by Anthony Farrar-Hockley, then chief of staff at Sandhurst but previously a Captain during the Korean war who had been captured along with his regiment and subjected to brainwashing by Chinese and Russian advisors, with the aim of making them confess to being 'Imperial Aggressors'. The fact that Farrar-Hockley had resisted the treatment, reinforced the message of the film. In contrast to the more sadistic concentration camp movies, CAPTURED has a positive message. Although Dobie is the main recipient of the torture, he also emerges as a charismatic figure among the other prisoners, reinforcing the message that they must stick together in resisting their captors.

One of the techniques used by the Chinese and Russians is a 'divide and rule' tactic. Identifying prisoners' weak spots and encouraging them to turn against each other. Dobie counters the technique by appealing to basic discipline and exhorting the prisoners to stick together. Even though he has been betrayed, Dobie says that's something the betrayer will have to live with afterwards, but for now it's important that they present a common front. The fact that Dobie is a corporal, rather than an officer, emphasises the concept that his behaviour is something that should be deep-rooted in every soldier and not just something that has to be instilled by an officer.

As a training film, CAPTURED is never quite as harrowing as something like THE CAMP ON BLOOD ISLAND. Krish uses voiceover to convey how Dobie's character is resisting the harsh treatment (being forced to sit upright for days in an unlit cell) although towards the end, there is an unsettling moment when Dobie begins to hallucinate hearing his parent's voices. When it comes to the most unsettling scene, where Dobie is waterboarded, we don't hear his thoughts, and just see him struggling as water is poured over a cloth held over his face.

CAPTURED is available as part of the British Film Institute 'Flipside' range and comes together with some of John Krish's memorable public information films (such as 'Sewing Machine' from 1973, where we see the last minute of a little girl's life before she's run over by a car, while her mother tries to finish her sewing) and a recruitment film made in 1976 for the Prison Service.

Gazette: The Old Folks at Home (Yorkshire TV, 26 August 1968)

Writer James Doran Director Tony Wickert

If Gazette is remembered today, it's as the series in which Gerald Harper made his first appearance as James Hadleigh. But in another context, it's an interesting example of "what might have been" in the wake of The Power Game. After two years starring in the BBC's Adam Adamant Lives, Gerald Harper was exhausted and open to the idea of taking part in an ensemble piece where he only had a few scenes in each episode. The series was set in a format similar to The Plane Makers instead of works manager Arthur Sugden trying to build planes against the antagonism of managing director John Wilder, Gazette pitted editor Frank Walters (Jon Laurimore) against newspaper owner James Hadleigh.

Gazette was the first drama series from Yorkshire TV, which began broadcasting on 29 July 1968. Before then Northern ITV had been Manchester-based (ABC in the weekends and Granada during the week) as had BBC programming "for the North". Yorkshire TV was a bold new concept (ironically, Patrick Wymark had been an artistic consultant for one of the rival bids for the franchise) to encourage economic growth. As Austin Mitchell puts it in his memoir Calendar Boy (2014)*, Yorkshire industries, "were still producing powerfully, but they were in slow decline…international competition intensified and the consequences of British complacency, our reluctance to invest and the inefficiencies of family capitalism came through."

Drama from Yorkshire TV was to reflect this new pride.In the second episode Turn A Blind Eye written by James Doran, Hadleigh's uncle Colonel Chamberlayne (Ralph Michael) tells him that the local hotel has poached a chef from Claridges. When Hadleigh queries how they can pay competitive wages, Chamberlayne tells him, "There's plenty of money up here these days and taste for good things. We're gradually turning away from London. Yorkshire nationalists, if you like. We no longer want to spend our money in the Big City." Hadleigh's return to Yorkshire is the subject of the opening episode of Gazette written by Elwyn Jones (Z Cars). The Westdale Gazette is inherited by James Hadleigh on the death of his father. When a rival newspaper prints a story that Hadleigh has resigned from his senior job in the Civil Service and is returning to Yorkshire, Editor Frank Walters (Jon Laurimore) is enraged that their own proprietor has given a story to a competitor. He phones Hadleigh in London to ask for a quote, "Something along the lines of I have decided that the future of England does not depend upon London ..." Hadleigh replies that he would never say anything so fatuous or trite but tells Walters, "I'm returning to Yorkshire to devote my attention to the complex of interests for which I now find myself responsible." His interests include a share of an engineering firm and his country estate.

Walters is suspicious as to why Hadleigh has given up his position as Assistant Secretary at the Department of Economic Planning. A subsequent episode will show

28

that Hadleigh's career hit a barrier after having an affair with the wife (Adrienne Corri) of a Government minister, but in the opening episode his motives for returning to Yorkshire are questioned. The Gazette's legal advisor asks Walters why he left Fleet Street to edit a provincial weekly. When Walters replies that, "I was sick to the stomach of London..driving two hours to work or getting off a packed train as greased as a sardine," the solicitor suggests Hadleigh may feel the same. Set up as men with similar motivations (both want to achieve something), Hadleigh and Walters end the first episode in a state of truce. Saddled with death duties, Hadleigh can't afford to sack the editor (his contract guarantees him three years wages on termination).

While Gazette reflected Yorkshire pride, it wasn't blind to the shortcomings of the region. Austin Mitchell points out that after Yorkshire TV's license was granted in June 1967, it was faced with the task of building a studio on, ", "a weed covered field where, a few years before, rows of slum terrace houses had sat less than a mile from the city centre (just far enough to make Leeds taxi businesses profitable when TV started)." The new studio was still unfinished when transmissions began in 1968 and staff had to be accommodated in an abandoned Burton's trouser factory next door, from where they could contemplate, "grime-covered factories like Yorkshire Screw…and rows of terraced housing rising from Cardigan Road behind and beyond the 'Lowry-style' railway arches to the west."

The Old Folks At Home reflects some of that disparity. It brings together Ralph Michael from The Power Game with Wendy Gifford and Elizabeth Begley from The Plane Makers. Hadleigh's uncle Colonel Chamberlayne (Michael) is chairman of Governors at Deepdeene School and tells Walters that he's under considerable pressure to sack the headmistress Georgina Barrett (Wendy Gifford). She's been sending her sixth form girls out to help deprived pensioners causing parents to complain that's not what they're paying £150 a term for. "They don't want their daughters exposed to all the sordid goings on of these people." It's been brought to a head by one of the girls complaining that she's been assaulted.

Walters sends Bill Spence to interview the headmistress. Leeds-born RADA graduate Michael Blackham had previously done a six month stint in Coronation Street as a suitor of the hapless Emily Nugent (Eileen Derbyshire) and was very much in the Simon Oates school of acting as the passionate lead reporter, still in occasional need of reigning-in by the Editor (perhaps tellingly, Gillian Wray as reporter Sue Jackson is absent from this story - more on that later). Part of the unpredictability of James Doran's script is that instead of making a play for her, Spence falls under her intellectual spell. She tells Spence that Deepdeene was founded to give the daughters of uncouth mill owners enough social graces to pick up a Lord for a husband. In the six months that she's been here Miss Barrett started the social work to make the girls aware of how the old, the poor and helpless live. "To enlarge their sympathies so they can make their own enlightened choices and not reflect the blinkered views of their parents. That's what education's for."

She refuses to disclose the name of the girl who claims to have been assaulted, telling Spence she doesn't believe the story. She says the girl is unhappy both at home and school and doesn't like social work because she's not interested in other people. Miss Barrett says she reluctantly reported the complaint to the police, but they spoke to the girl and took no further action. As far as Miss Barrett is concerned that's the end of the matter.

Spence is convinced the Gazette should support Miss Barrett but Walters demands to know more: "She's an attractive woman. Why isn't she married? Is there a man in her life? It's important to know! Is she a well-balanced normal woman who wants, purely as a teacher to improve the standing of her school…or a frustrated lesbian bent on ruining the lives of adolescent girls?"

However, Georgina Barrett is a determined operator. She adopted a submissive front with Spence, but also arranges to have dinner at the local hotel with her old friend James Hadleigh. She compliments Hadleigh on arranging a special meal four hours in advance. Hadleigh says It pays off, because it makes the restaurant take trouble. But he also returns the compliment saying, "You're one of the few women I know who'd appreciate it." Hadleigh agrees to intercede with his uncle ("a nice but very stupid man")to ensure the Governors will not sack her. Chamberlayne agrees that if the Gazette investigates the alleged assault and Hadleigh makes a decision based on their findings, he will be guided by Hadleigh.

The next day, Spence has arranged to accompany model pupil Julia Gill (Diane Mercer) on her rounds. She tells him the social work is a bit of a drag. "I'd rather be doing something about Vietnam, .being a nurse (for) all those poor children being burned and wounded with no-one to look after them."

After a pleasant visit to the arthritis-ridden Mrs Wright (Winifred Dennis) they move on to a cobbled street of back-to-back terraces which appears to have been filmed in the soon-to-be demolished Prosperity Street. In a cold squalid room, they find Mrs Parsons (Elizabeth Begley) huddled in bed.

When Julia asks if she wants the window open, Mrs Parsons snaps, "No it's cold. You feel the cold when you're old." As Spence puts a shilling in the meter for the gas fire he asks. "Don't you mind the mess love?" She snaps back that, "Nobody else cares, why should I?" She tells Spence she lives on four pounds ten a week (about £78 in 2018) and a pound of that goes on rent. Spence asks if she's got any family. A pained look passes over her bitter face, "Aye. Three boys. Two girls. Troubles enough of their own without me adding to them. So they keep telling me." Spence asks, what about the Social Security. "It's not up to them to help me, " Mrs Parsons shoots back, and when Spence asks who it is up to she replies, "Them that owe it to me. They don't want me! They don't like me!"

Mrs Parsons tells them to leave saying that, "kindness is never free they all want something in return. Money, gratitude, love, something for nothing. Makes them feel superior. Looking at a dirty old bitch like me makes anyone feel superior." Despite her harsh reception, Julia tells Spence she will go back because she's stubborn.

Meanwhile, after Spence has tricked the name of the girl who made the assault allegation out of Julia, Walters accepts Hadleigh's challenge to investigate the claim. Her mother (Hilary Mason) confirms to Walters that she disagrees with the idea of social work. "I came from those slums, so did my husband. We fought our way out of it . The rest of those people didn't fight. They were full of grumbles but deep down they liked it. They were cosy like pigs in muck." Although her daughter Audrey will miss her exams, her mother say she doesn't need them. " She'll never have to work. All that matters is that she mixes with the right kind of people."

When Walters interviews the brash and condescending Audrey (Ann Holloway, later one of Patrick Cargill's daughters in Father Dear Father) she laughingly confirms that the pensioner, "..tried to goose me. I gave him a good hard slap across his dribbly old chops and ran. I hate old people. I think they should all be put out of their misery when they're 60."

Finally, Walters convinces the grimy and suspicious Jacko Pendlebury (Joe Gladwin) to admit him to the clutter of his house. Jacko needs convincing that Walters is not from the Welfare, who are always trying to put him in a home. "This is me home," he tells Walters, gesturing to the array of scattered furniture and disassembled TV's. "I bought it 45 years ago. It's been me castle since wife died." Jacko gleefully tells Walters he spends his time betting on horses " I'm only old age pensioner round these parts who can afford to drink every night." When Walters asks him about Audrey, Jacko gleefully recalls she was a pretty one and admits goosing Audrey to frighten her away, "They're very cunning these welfare people. Thought they could get at me with that one and get me put away." Walters concludes he's an old reprobate and walks out as Jacko shouts after him to make sure that if they send any more from the welfare, make sure they're pretty ones.

Walters shows Hadleigh a report quoting Audrey Miller as saying, "the shock she experienced lasted only a couple of seconds. Her main objection seems to be the age and unattractiveness of her attacker". Hadleigh is outraged, saying they can't print this, the parents will sue. Walters agrees but says if they do, they'll lose. He then shows Hadleigh a second more sober and discrete version of the report. He tells Hadleigh the first version is to pass on to Colonel Chamberlayne. It's what he'll publish if the Governors sack Miss Barrett. Hadleigh departs saying he'll enjoy watching his uncle read the story.

Tony Doran was one of the two credited writers on The Ipcress File (1965) and like series creator Robert Barr and script editor Elwyn Jones, Doran had previously worked on the BBC's Z Cars. After exploring the new money and "Yorkshire independence" in his previous episode, Doran looked at those left behind of the gold rush in this story. Although Mrs Wright is the most affable of the three pensioners, we still catch a disappointed look on Winifred Dennis' face as Julia and Spence rush off to their next appointment. In fifty years, nothing much has changed - the greatest social service that can be provided to pensioners is company. Both she and Mrs Parsons have children, but they've moved away and have no time for their parents. This was the inevitable consequence of children feeling they have to move away from their home to make a success of their life and was another of the social economic effects which the founding of Yorkshire Television hoped to counteract.

Director Tony Wickert pulls a fast-moving episode together with some fine guest performances from Elizabeth Begley as the bitter Mrs Parsons, and Joe Gladwin* as the hedonistic Jacko, and solid leads from the waspish Harper and the world-weary Laurimore.

It's fair to say there's no sugar-coating in this episode. Mrs Miller and her daughter are equally as selfish and spiteful as Mrs Parsons but the charming and idealistic Miss Barrett is also shown to have been too ready to disbelieve Audrey's story. The fact that Audrey was brash enough to have been unscarred by the incident, and Jacko claims to have made the assault only to scare her off seems like a bit of special pleading. And not too convincing given Jacko's final words.

To put this in context, Gazette's sexual politics are firmly those of the 1960's. In Elwyn Jones' opening episode Gillian Wray's reporter Sue Jackson tells Hadleigh she wears her short (not mini) skirt to the police station because they're a bunch of "dirty bastards" who'll give her more information when they see her legs. Later on Hadleigh's uncle Colonel Chamberlayne jokes with Walters that Sue "resisted my advances" and Walters replies "She resists mine too!" At the end of the episode, Walters tells Spence that since Sue won't co-operate, "let's put the paper to bed instead." The series is very much of its time. To return to Austin Mitchell again, he tells the story of a new recruit to Yorkshire TV who brought his wife up from London to show her round Leeds. They went into a pub for a drink and ordered two pints of beer, but when the barman realised who it was for, he snatched one of the glasses back saying, "We don't serve pints to Ladies!"

Gazette was hindered by being transmitted during the "false start" of the new ITV. There was antagonism between the old and new TV contractors. While Yorkshire Tv put Gazette out at 9pm on Friday Evenings, other companies such as Anglia TV preferred to follow London Weekend Television in screening Frost On Friday at 9pm with Gazette relegated to 11pm. It's rumoured that ATV only showed Gazette at 9pm because Lew Grade resented David Frost and LWT taking over ATV's lucrative London weekend franchise. As if this wasn't bad enough, all the ITV companies were hit by technicians strikes over the new colour TV technology and some scheduled programmes were not even shown at all.

Perhaps unsurprisingly, once the ITV network had settled down, Yorkshire TV decided that Gazette had run its course, but Gerald Harper and Gillian Wray would return in Hadleigh, a series focussing on the title character's wider business interests.

*Coincidentally, Michael Blackham and Joe Gladwin had worked together during the 1965 Summer Season at Blackpool's Grand Theatre. My Perfect Husband traded on the success of the BBC's Meet The Wife with Thora Bird and Freddie Frinton starring As Dolores and Fred Fazackerley. Michael Blackham played their son, Sebastian and Joe Gladwin played Hercules Shorthouse. The cast also included Marti Webb and Diane (Hi-Di-Hi) Holland.

*Calendar Boy by Austin Mitchell, Pen and Sword Books 2014

The Power Game at Hammer Films

Sir John Wilder (Patrick Wymark), lead character in "The Power Game" , borrowed some of his characteristics from real-life captains' of industry. Did Hammer Films' Carreras family inspire the fiery relationship between his adversary Caswell Bligh and his son Kenneth?

In his memoir "High Drama" , Rex Firkin, producer of "The Plane Makers" and " The Power Game" mentions three inspirations for the character of Sir John Wilder (Patrick Wymark). Since Wilder began in "The Plane Makers" it's not surprising that one was Sir Basil Smallpeice, managing director of British Overseas Airways Corporation, who cut losses and beat Pan Am to introducing transatlantic plane travel.

The second was Sir John Davis, autocratic managing director of the Rank Organisation, (who successfully weathered the British film industry depression by diversifying into other areas such as backing the prototype photocopier - Rank Xerox.). The third was literary agent A.D.Peters, who was married to actress Margot Grahame (The Informer, The Crimson Pirate) but would spend every weekend in Lewes with his girlfriend. ("Wife and mistress both knew about each other. They didn't complain. They lived their lives quite separately.").

"The Power Game" saw Wilder becoming joint managing director of Bligh Construction, the family firm run by Caswell Bligh (Clifford Evans) and his son Kenneth Bligh (Peter Barkworth). Part of Wilder's strategy was to wrest control of the company by exploiting the toxic relationship between the Blighs. The question is whether the Bligh's had a real-life inspiration and whether part of this was Hammer Films' Carreras family?

Hammer Films is best known for its horror movies such as "Curse of Frankenstein" and "Dracula" starring Peter Cushing and Christopher Lee. Clifford Evans starred in two Hammer productions – "Curse of the Werewolf" (1960) in which he played Oliver Reed's foster father and Kiss of the Vampire (1962) in which he played the Van Helsing substitute Professor Zimmer. Hammer films was a family firm, run during the 1950's and 60's by "Lieutenant Colonel" James Carreras and his son Michael Carreras. James was an ex-car salesman and natural deal-maker in the Lew Grade mode. Much of the early success of Hammer Films can be attributed to his knack of securing funding from American studios – often on the back of nothing more than the title and a lurid poster. Carreras Senior enjoyed socialising through his work with the Variety Club charity. While it is sometimes said that he used the proceeds from Hammer to finance his charity work, it's undeniable that the Variety Club also allowed him to mix with the highest levels of British film finance and distribution, thus ensuring a steady flow of order for Hammer. The Variety Club also provides another Wilder connection; Carreras met Josephine Douglas, director of the Plane Makers episode "A Question of Supply" through the Variety Club (An experienced TV producer – "6.5 Special", "Emergency Ward 10" -Douglas later landed a job as line producer for Dracula AD 1972).

His son, Michael Carreras was arguably more of a film fan than a deal-maker. Unlike his father, who took little interest in production matters, Michael Carreras quickly began producing and directing fillers (including one featuring Cyril Stapleton and the Showband (1955) - who would later record the 1967 theme to The Power Game). Although he enthusiastically moved to directing thrillers, he wanted Hammer to broaden its horizons past horror films. He tried to break away with his own production company in December 1960. Capricorn Productions made only two movies – The Savage Guns, and What A Crazy World, before Michael returned to Hammer in 1963.

In a fascinating article in " Little Shoppe of Horrors" 13 (1996) Denis Meikle argues that Capricorn Films was undermined by, "a closed shop operated by a coterie of luncheon-clubbers" who "had set their faces against any involvement with the 'ungrateful' son of a friend and fellow Variety Clubber. For fear of offending the man who maintained powerful allies in the US and who was still supplying much of their more popular product."

On TV, the Bligh family was introduced in the first episode of "The Power Game" . Sir John Wilder, having left the aircraft industry, was looking for new challenges. He was sitting on the board of a merchant bank that was looking to invest in the Bligh Construction firm and needed to put their own man in as joint managing director.

Publicity for the TV show says Caswell Bligh left school at 14 to join his father's firm in Preston making tombstones. Caswell built up the business, winning local government contracts for paving stones by fixing the Clerk of Works. He further increased the company's profitability by some dodgy dealing while building American airbases during the second world war. Bligh later joined the Royal Engineers winning the rank of Lieutenant-Colonel (Carreras, it should be noted, was educated at Manchester Grammar School, promoted to Lt-Col while serving in the Honourable Artillery Company and awarded the MBE for his service in the defence of London. It was after the war that he began winning finance from America that lay the foundations of Hammer Films.)

In the first episode of "The Power Game", Bligh is resistant to any attempt to diminish his control of the Bligh Construction, despite the fact that he spends much of his time and resources as a member of the National Export Board. Bligh is lobbying for the government to create a "Ministry of Roads" with himself as Minister overseeing a massive expansion in motorway construction.

Wilder convinces Bligh to accept him when he points out that Bligh's son Kenneth (Peter Barkworth) wants control of the company. "He doesn't know it yet. He's got to cut somebody's throat to do it. Yours -or mine – if I'm here."

Ken Bligh is portrayed by Peter Barkworth as frustrated. He is haunted by a reputation for having underpriced bids on early construction projects, although in one episode ("Late Via Rome") Ken exploits his reputation for bungling bids to fool a business partner into thinking a project is going to be a disaster and trick them into pulling out . Ken is also frustrated by Caswell's refusal to try new ideas. In "The Big View" Ken tells him. "You only ever think of your own image. You never think, 'is it a workable idea? Is it suitable for requirements?' Only, 'has it ever been done before?' Nasty new idea! How's Bligh's going to look?"

At the end of the 1966 series, Ken sells his shares in Bligh Construction, and buys a sub-contracting company. Unfortunately, in his final 1969 episode ("The Heart Market") we learn that Ken has lost money on two more projects. Caswell's final verdict is that he was never cut out for business and should have been a parson or a schoolmaster. The irony is that Bligh would never have tolerated Ken being a success. Caswell fills his board of directors with "yes-men" and constantly interferes in projects that Ken has set up. As Wilder tells Caswell in "Standard Practice" "To see him standing on his own two feet would have knocked you off your own!"

So were the Bligh's based on the Carreras family? We will probably never know. Power Game writer Edmund Ward had a background in the construction industry (later exploited in his series "The Hanged Man" starring Colin Blakely) and it's possible that such an adversarial relationship existed in many other British family firms. It's also fair to acknowledge that once he'd won the finance for his movies, James Carreras did not interfere in production. However, there are similarities. Both James Carreras and Caswell Bligh started out in the North East and turned a small family firm into a powerhouse.

Both Caswell Bligh and James Carreras wanted to stick to a winning formula – British public works for Bligh, American-backed horror films for Carreras. Both sons wanted to do something different – Ken Bligh wanting to win construction projects in Africa, while Michael Carreras wanted to make musicals and big budget epics.

In "The Power Game" Ken Bligh's fatal flaw is implied to be his honesty (or credulity) in a world where everyone is lying. And in real life, Michael Carreras attempt to set up his own film company seems to have been undermined because the market was already stacked against him.

In the end we have to remember that Rex Firkin said there were at least three inspirations for Sir John Wilder. So even if the Bligh's did have something of the Carreras family in them, there may have been other inspirations too. And any

36

inspiration is just a starting point. Once an actor is a success –as both Clifford Evans and Peter Barkworth were – the writers start adjusting for the nuances they bring. And the characters are still merely puppets moving in the direction the Script Editor wants the story to go.

Still, there was one final twist worthy of Caswell Bligh himself.

In 1972, Michael Carreras learned that his father was negotiating to sell Hammer Films to its rival Tigon Films. There was nothing in the agreement to guarantee Michael's position as managing director so, in order to secure his future, he took out a loan from the ICI Pension Fund to buy the company, thinking agreements were in place with British distributors to develop new movies. Unfortunately, he found that all he had bought was a name. Many distributors were no longer willing to honour agreements made with Sir James - even those with whom James Carreras now had a contract as a consultant. Although Michael Carreras soldiered on for several more years, it must have seemed like history repeating itself. *

*Source: Hammer Films: The Elstree Studios Years by Wayne Kinsey.

The Net (1953)

Released seven months after David Lean's *The Sound Barrier*, the quest for supersonic flight is taken to the next level in *The Net*. Professor Heathley (James Donald - *Quatermass and the Pit*) leads a project at the Port Amberley research establishment to develop an atomic powered, faster-than-sound jet. Heathley sees this as just an intermediate stage before space travel. Heathley wants to pilot the test flight himself, but the project Director (Maurice Denham) insists that the jet should fly under the ground control of Alex Leon (Herbert Lom). When the Director dies under suspicious circumstances, security chief Sam Seagram (Robert Beatty) must decide if it's an accident or enemy action.

Directed by Anthony Asquith, *The Net* is based on a 1952 novel by poet and journalist John Pudney, whose poem *For Johnny* ("Do not despair, for Johnny-Head-In-Air..") had featured significantly in Asquith's 1945 movie *The Way To The Stars* (to the extent that it inspired the film's US title *Johnny In The Clouds*). Pudney had been a wartime RAF intelligence officer, and editor of Odhams *News Review* until 1950, which may have given him a dual insight into the security leaks at Britain's post war Atomic Energy Establishment. In a note at the beginning of *The Net* Pudney apologises to Britain's scientists and research workers, assuring them that, *"Real people and actual projects are necessarily excluded from this otherwise true tale."*

As in *The Plane Makers*, both the book and the film deal principally with the tensions between the project workers, but the film does feature the M7 jet flying in several scenes. Launched, like a seaplane from water, the jet roars over the base, scattering the surrounding birds before increasing to Mach 1 and the sound barrier. The special effects are credited to Pinewood's head of visual effects Bill Warrington, Bryan Langley and Albert Whitlock. It appears that a combination of techniques were used to bring the atomic jet to life: a sleek model (designed or at least supervised by Warrington, who won an Oscar for *The Guns of Navarone*), Matte paintings by Whitlock integrating the imagined base with live action, and blue screen travelling mattes by Langley.

The shots of the M7 in flight seem both primitive and ahead-of-their time. Obviously fake but impressionistic with visible trails depicting the fast-than-sound flight.The design of the M7 is remarkable in that it's not too different from supersonic jets being trialled in the 21st century.

William Fairchild's script is generally faithful to Pudney's novel but makes some changes in the interests of condensing a 300 page book down to an 80 minute movie. There is also an interesting bit of personalisation. In the novel, Heathley - like *Inspector Morse* is referred to only by his last name, even by his wife. In the movie, James Donald's character is called Michael and the call-sign of the M7 jet becomes *"Mike Seven"*. emphasising his obsession with the project.

Pudney makes reference early in the novel to atom scientist Bruno Pontecorvo, who defected to the Soviet Union in 1950, and Klaus Fuchs, convicted of spying in the same year. This suggests that Pudney's model for Port Amberley was the Atomic Energy Research Establishment at Harwell, set (like Port Amberley) in an isolated agricultural community. Pudney's concern would appear to be the twin pressures of life in an isolated community where there is no escape from work and no-one can discuss their work. As one character says, "they're living and working in a synthetic cell in the very midst of an old, steady civilisation."

Pudney gives a clue to the meaning of his title, *The Net* with a 17th century epigram by John Northbrooke about hornets flying through a net that catches small flies. In other words, security measures stop accidental breaches but don't always deter a sustained attack. The net of secrecy, where no-one can discuss their work, can also strain personal relations. In the movie, the opening minutes show James Donald referring to the bureaucratic constraints imposed by the Director, holding his hand up to the fence of the research establishment as he tells Maurice Denham, "You keep me in a nice strong net. One day you'll find all you've got is an obsolete machine and a fossilised scientist."

The emotional net also stifles Heathley's wife Lydia (Phyllis Calvert). Pudney's novel explores Lydia's frustration with *"the withdrawn, secretive element inf Heathley's character which was so obsessed with power that it made him say he could not afford to worry.".* The book covers this in much greater depth than the movie, opening with Lydia contemplating adultery - at first just generally and then responding in particular to the flirtation of Alex Leon (Herbert Lom). *"Her passion for Alex cried out for atonement or fulfilment...(the affair) had been a liberation in itself (from) the prison of which Heathley seemed still so unaware."*

In both the book and the film, Heathley's desire to pilot the jet on its test flight is opposed by the deputy Director (just, *the Director* in the movie). Heathley regards the M7 as just a stepping stone to the M8 which will taken them into space, and is frustrated by the slow and steady methods of his supervisor. When the Director is killed, Heathley misrepresents their last conversation, claiming that he was coming round to Heathley's point of view and pushes through the manned test flight.

Following the prologue between Heathley and the Director, Fairchild makes a similarly speedy and effective introduction of the cast during a party thrown by Lydia. The multi-national scientists and technicians are united in a session singing, *Ten Green Bottles* led by Dennis Bord (Noel Willman). Fairchild's use of this song is ironic, not just because it allows the Director (Maurice Denham)to underline the risk of letting his project leader make a test flight (prodding him in the chest and repeating, "If one green bottle, should accidentally fall...") but because it anticipates the fate of the director himself.

The introduction of Dennis Bord (Noel Willman) marks the most significant change between book and film. In Pudney's novel, Dennis Bord is the security chief and

Seagram is a visiting liaison from Washington. In the movie, Seagram is the *Canadian* security chief, while Bord becomes a medical doctor responsible for the pressure suits used by the pilots of the M7. In both book and film, Bord is a traitor. Pudney allows the reader to discover this gradually, whereas the film audience knows there is something odd about Bord within the first ten minutes. The Director confides to Bord that he's not going to let Heathley fly the M7, hoping the Doctor can watch Heathley for signs of strain. We see Bord spinning an ornamental globe as the director's words echo in his head. He spins the globe faster and faster as Benjamin Frankel's initially twinkling music grows in intensity and merges with the roar of an engine test. Soon afterwards we learn that the director has been injured in a fall. This is the same sequence of events as in the novel, but because Fairchild has made Bord a doctor, the deputy's death becomes less ambiguous. In the medical centre, Bord prepares to administer a life-saving injection. But then Bord squirts the syringe of adrenalin into a cloth and then holds a mirror over the director's mouth. We see Bord's cold eyes reflected in the mirror, as the director's breath clouds the glass and then dies away. Bord calls the security officer, Seagram (Robert Beatty) and tells him the director's heart, "didn't respond to the injection."

In the novel, Bord runs a small spy network, briefing one agent over a game of billiards at the village Constitutional Club and receiving messages in matchboxes from "Jose, one of the Oceanic bartenders, under the impression that he was working for the British secret service." In the movie, Fairchild abbreviates this to a scene of Bord calling for a drink at the village pub. Bord puts his newspaper on the bar and glances significantly at a pipe-smoking gent who says, "'Scuse me, you've left your paper. Mind if I read it?" and pockets the newspaper.

In both novel and film, Bord's ultimate aim is to take both Heathley and the M7 over the Iron Curtain. Pudney says that, *"Bord was not in his own eyes a traitor.In order to betray, a man must have allegiances, and he lacked them all. Not only the conventional loyalties to King and country, to kith and kin, but the deeper allegiances to God, to people, to a way of life. Dennis Bord had..stripped himself of all of these..War service had tempered his courage, educated his sense of violence and affirmed his nihilistic detachment from people and situations."."*

By the time Pudney's novel was published, the diplomats Burgess and Maclean had already defected to Russia, although MI6 traitor Kim Philby had not yet been exposed. Pudney's characterisation of his 'hornet' Bord as being in charge of security is therefore more reflective of the times. So too is the character of Sam Seagram, the Texan called in from Washington to scrutize British procedures. By 1951, the 'special relationship' between America and Britain saw the United Kingdom as the aged, infirm, impoverished and slightly dotty parent that needed careful supervison.

By changing Bord to a doctor, Fairchild removes these disquieting undertones of national humiliation. Instead of being an intimidating security officer, Bord is a genial doctor. A trusted member of the project design team, he also goes out into the community, treating the ailing father of technician Brian Jackson. Noel Willman, who would later play Doctor Ravna in Hammer's *Kiss of the Vampire* presents Bord with a superficial charm which occasionally drops to reveal the coldness beneath. In both book and film, Bord exploits betrayals by Heathley's wife Lydia, and assistant Brian Jackson to push Heathley towards a crisis point.

In the role of Lydia Heathley, Phyllis Calvert was re-united with Anthony Asquith who had directed her onstage opposite Jack Watling in Terence Rattigan's 1942 play *Flare Path**. Calvert's character had been at the centre of a love triangle, and since she often played the more boring 'good girl' parts in movies, the role of Lydia might have been an attempt to revisit that stage success.

In both book and film, Lydia Heathley (Phyllis Calvert) spends an afternoon on nearby Flimby Pier with Alex Leon (Herbert Lom) where they share a kiss. Pudney's novel goes into much more depth about Lydia's resulting guilt whereas in the movie both Alex and Lydia realise it was a bad idea that shouldn't be taken much further. Pudney's novel portrays Alex a former concentration camp inmate who lives for the moment. *"If Alex appeared too anxious to be considered an ordinary man of the world, it might well have been because he had emerged from unspeakable darknesses of body and mind, fighting every inch of the way."*. Herbert Lom portrays Alex as likeable and Fairchild invents a tense scene in which he clearly thinks Heathley is about to confront him over his liaison with Lydia, only to realise that Heathley is more concerned that Brian Jackson has agreed to copilot the jet out of misplaced loyalty. Lom's evident relief justifies the truncated nature of his romance with Lydia.

In the novel, Alex has a sister, Ilse who has also *"been in the hands of the secret police before"*, leading her to fear Bord with his penetrating hypnotic eyes. Pudney depicts Ilse as a strong contrast to the vapoury Anglo Saxon Lydia. In a conference, he picks out Ilse, "whose warm colouring defied the tobacco haze." Ilse is suspected of treachery by both Heathley and Seagram, but it eventually transpires that her mysterious behaviour is due to a manipulative relationship with the late deputy Director. Just as Lydia feels Alex has "let her out of her prison", the Deputy thinks Ilse has had a transformative effect on his life. *"The deputy made a specialty of hating women. I looked on that as a challenge. He had been unhappily married twice. I felt sorry for him. That was what he wanted."* We learn that on the night of his accident, the heavy-drinking deputy Director had asked Ilse to go away with him, saying she was the only person who could stop him drinking. Ilse didn't want to be his protector and had walked out when the deputy started to get abusive. That was just before his fatal accident, meaning she was the last person to see him.

Not surprisingly, this entire sub-plot disappears from the movie and Ilse becomes Caroline Cartier (Muriel Pavlow - *Reach for The Sky*) - a French scientist unrelated to Alex Leon. Caroline retains Ilse's stronger characteristics, standing up to Heathley when he proposes a manned flight of the M7, but loses the femme fatale qualities. Like Ilse, Caroline is the love interest for Brian Jackson (Patric Doonan), a local scholarship boy from the village who is Heathley's protege and second-in-command. It is Brian who co-pilots the M7 on the first test-flight - a test that almost proves fatal when Heathley blacks out due to G forces while turning at twice the speed of sound. Being younger and quicker to recover, Brian is able to flick on the switch which accepts the ground-control signal and save the jet from crashing.

Brian represents solid English values. Fairchild's script reproduces a scene from the novel in which Brian's father lies dying in his bedroom in the village. He expresses a wish to be taken downstairs before he dies, because the stairs are too narrow for a coffin. "I don't want to go out in a box through the window like my dad, with a rickyard rope and tackle." There's an almost Thomas Hardy overtone to George Jackson's wish to die downstairs. He dies, just after moving downstairs. In the movie we're told that old George was proud to have walked downstairs by himself. In both book and film, George Jackson dies while his son is co-piloting the M7 jet.

Pudney takes an ambiguous approach to the stolid Englishman. He notes that the security guards, "were simple, slightly underpaid, family men of great integrity. They might have served as sentries at Agincourt, at Bannockburn, at Waterloo or at Caen. They looked for a recognised enemy or an overt act. History was on their side, after all" Similarly Lydia's mother deprecates Major Seagram's theory that "fatal illusions" may cut through the net of security. *"I was brought up in a world in which you sacked a man who was a cad, but you put a traitor up against a wall and shot him whether he had illusions or not. And what was the result? I can recall precious few traitors"* But when Sir Charles Cruddock (Walter Fitzgerald) appoints Brian as the new deputy director he does so because he knows Brian will be easy to control. *"He'll take instructions from me and I'll trust him to carry out our policy."* Brian's acceptance and the ban of manned tests of the M7 is the final 'betrayal' which Bord uses to provoke Heathley.

Pudney shows Bord manipulating Heathley. *'The eyes focussed with prophetic fervour, "A man like yourself bears responsibility for millions of human beings. Your power rises above such thing. It is the duty of a man like yourself to consider your potential not just in terms of..a country which is too small for your ideas."'*. Heathley is swayed by the argument, reflecting that *'It was almost as if some part of himself had used the lips of another man to form the words which he had never dared to speak."*

In the movie, these 'fatal illusions' are removed from Donald's character. Bord - as a member of the design team - agrees to help Heathley take the M7 on an unathorised test flight but does not reveal himself until they have successfully completed the test manouevres. Bord tells Heathley to fly the jet East saying, *"We'll show those little people at Port Amberley they can't control people like us. I've been promised complete control from now on. We'll make the decisions. Where we're going, power will be ours!"*

Throughout the movie, Bord has appeared obsessed with Heathley and his final speech might open the way for the inevitable speculation of gay undertones. Fairchild and Asquith encourage this speculation with the earlier scene in which Alex Leon thinks Heathley has discovered his affair with Lydia. The professor surprises him by saying that he's feeling guilty about his exploitation of Brian Jackson's loyalty, which is "a kind of love!" Is Heathley's indifference to Lydia really caused by his obsession with the M7 or his fascination with the younger man? Does Bord want to fly Heathley and the M7 somewhere over the rainbow? John Pudney notes that Bord's, *"tastes in personal relationships, when they were not conventional, were coarse and a little dangerous."* and he remarks upon *"The nature which had lavished lust on him, but denied him love."* That certainly sounds like a pre-Wolfenden Report nod towards Bord's sexuality. The establishment view was that homosexuals were a security risk because they were open to blackmail (mainly because of society and the law's attitudes) but Pudney seems to see Bord's nihilism as rooted in his sexuality.

In the movie, Bord pulls a gun on Heathley when he refuses to fly east. Heathley pulls an aerobatic manoeuvre that forces Bord to drop the gun and then as Bord is reaching for the weapon, his oxygen pipe comes unfastened. Willman's face distorts in horror as he realises what's happened and his terrified shrieks echo over the intercome in the control room before he suffocates. In the novel, Pudney depicts the end as a struggle with Satan. Heathley realises for the first time that Bord has been setting him up when he admits to killing the Deputy. *"There's only one power in the world. The controlled power of humanity, controlled by men of destiny like you and me."* At that point, Lydia's voice comes over the intercom telling Heathley she loves him and not to believe any rumours he's heard about her silly flirtation, *"in the eyes of God I remained faithful."* Bord threatens to kill Heathley who realises that he was crossing, *"the cruellest frontier of all - and beyond it the desert land without God, withoout love, without honour, where men killed you expediently and spoke casually of it."* Heathley tells Bord he's going to comply and then pulls the pressure line of his hood away from the panel which feeds it. *"The shining plastic of the hood sucked inward and wrapped itself around Bord's face as the pressure stove it in, suffocating him...the man had died mercifully and quickly in his moment of imagined triumph."*

In the novel, Heathley calmly lands the jet in "a taut sulky sea", throwing Bord's body into the water, *"He would face the music, but first he would dispose of the Devil."* Fairchild's script for the movie delivers a *James Bond* style coda. Bord's corpse falls across Heathley sending the jet into a death dive. Heathley pushes the body aside and regains control but once again G Forces overcome him. In the movie, it is Lydia calling over the intercom which rouses Heathley long enough for him to pull the jet into a stable pattern and bring the plane home.

The Net follows on from *The Sound Barrier* but with its science fiction overtones also anticipates the *Quatermass* films - particularly *Quatermass II* (1957) where the complex at Winnerden Flats seems like an extension of Port Amberley. There are also echoes of *The Net* in *Doppelganger*, not just because of the casting of Herbert Lom, but also because of the climactic scene with astronaut Roy Thinnes trying to establish the ground-control signal.

It's probably fair to say that *The Net* (both book and film) is a story about research and security that happens to feature a jet plane, rather than being about the aviation industry. Nevertheless, it does foreshadow *The Plane Makers* - particularly the third series with the introduction of David Corbett and the development of The Predator.

Flare Path was the basis for Asquith's movie **The Way To The Stars**, *which had made great use of John Pudney's poem 'For Johnny'. Rattigan teamed up with David Lean to script,* **The Sound Barrier**

The Shadow Knows...

The Shadow Russell Mulcahy's controversial 1994 movie about a supernatural crime fighter was re-released in 2015 as a "collector's edition" DVD/BluRay from Medium Rare. The film may have been considered a failure by Universal Studios, which hoped it would be the start of a movie "franchise" and also annoyed admirers of the character. But I admit I love this movie. Its virtues outweigh its sins.

The most dedicated fans of The Shadow follow the series of "pulp" magazine stories written by Walter B Gibson during the 1930's and 40's but I first came across "The Shadow" in Dennis O'Neil and Mike Kaluta's 1970's DC Comics. The romantic 1930's adventures depicted a small band of undercover agents fighting crime under the direction of a hawk-nosed black cloaked phantom. Despite the art deco setting, The Shadow reflected a contemporary 1970's taste for vigilante heroes (as Jim Steranko said, "The Shadow doesn't believe in the death penalty. He *is* the death penalty").

Inspired by the comics, I searched out more "Shadow" product but was confused to come across the 1960's Belmont novels in which he tackled a T.H.R.U.S.H style secret spy organisation, the 1960's Archie Comics in which he was a costumed superhero, and a radio script reproduced in an anthology called "The Great American Detective", in which Lamont Cranston was a Peter Wimsey-style detective with the ability to hypnotise villains into believing he was invisible. It wasn't until New English Library began reprinting Walter Gibson's original 1930's novels that I found the authentic Shadow.

For many viewers the first big problem with the 1994 movie is the origin of The Shadow presented by scriptwriter David Koepp (Jurassic Park, Carlito's Way). The movie opens in Tibet with Lamont Cranston (Alec Baldwin) as the corrupt leader of an opium peddling gang. With commendable brevity, Cranston is kidnapped by the servants of a Tibetan mystic, who proposes to use his powers of mind control to help Cranston control the darkness within him.

While contradicting the origin of The Shadow in the pulp magazines, Koepp's version does reflect aspects of origin stories given in the 1940's Shadow comics and Howard Chaykin's equally controversial and nihilistic 1986 mini-series for DC Comics. With the revelation that villain Shiwan Khan (John Lone) is a failed project of the Tibetan mystic, the movie also takes on overtones of Marvel Comics' Dr Strange(who battled Baron Mordo, evil student of his Tibetan mentor the Ancient One) overtones realised during a scene where Khan concentrates on the pattern of a wall tapestry and the pattern stretches out towards him like something Dr Strange creator Steve Ditko would draw.

For those who know the standard continuity of The Shadow from Walter B Gibson's magazine novels, this tampering with his origin can be a major irritant. But The Shadow has always been nebulous; a dream or a nightmare shaped by commercial demands. The Shadow started out as a radio drama narrator, something like the BBC's "Man in Black", created to promote a crime magazine from publishers Street & Smith. When readers started asking for a magazine featuring The Shadow the publishers hired magician Walter Gibson to give life to the voice. Under the house name of Maxwell Grant, Gibson spun tales of the black clad phantom waging war on criminals. If it owed something to Dracula and The Count of Monte Cristo, The Shadow also inspired a new genre of magazine and comic book followers such as The Phantom Detective and Batman and arguably also set the template for the Mission: Impossible TV show.

Ironically, the popularity of the magazine generated full-blown Shadow crime dramas on the Mutual Radio Network. Whereas Gibson's novels showed that Lamont Cranston was just one of many false identities used by former war hero and undercover agent Kent Allard, the radio series had to go for simplicity. For the mass audience Lamont Cranston , aided by girlfriend Margo Lane, was The Shadow – a detective using powers of mind control to "cloud men's minds". The popularity of the radio show eventually forced Gibson to backtrack on earlier novels (which suggested that former aviator Kent Allard was the Shadow) and concede that Lamont Cranston was the real identity of the cloaked crimefighter.

Like the then-recent "Batman" movie, "The Shadow" pulls together different aspects from the characters' history to create a new myth. In the movie, Lamont Cranston uses the power of his mind to warp his features into the characteristic carrion face of The Shadow. He is able to "cloud the minds of men" although in one scene his silhouette is pinned to a wall by a crossbow bolt, and the Shadow eerily morphs and materialises, shrugging off the cloak which remains pinned to the wall.

Alec Baldwin immaculately embodies the sardonic hero, archly capturing the commanding delivery of Gibson's novels ("I've saved your life", the Shadow tells Dr Roy Tam (Sab Shimono) early in the movie, "It now belongs to me. " This echoes The Shadow's orders to new recruit Cliff Marsland in the novel Mobsmen On The Spot ; "It is not your task to kill.. it is your task to wait and to obey.")

Fans of the novels may also be confounded by the pragmatic use of Margo Lane (Penelope Ann Miller) which departs from her literary origins but ironically puts her more firmly at the heart of the movie. Not only is the movie Margo psychic (making her a romantic equal to the predatory Cranston) she is also the daughter of scientist Reinhardt Lane (Ian McKellan) who is kidnapped by villain Shiwan Kahn (John Lone) in order to use his prototype atomic bomb to blackmail the city. Kahn, who appeared in four of the original novels is portrayed here as evil incarnate. Instead of trying to destroy The Shadow, Kahn tries to tempt him back to the way of darkness; "I would sooner destroy a Rembrandt than kill you" he tells Cranston.

As the new documentary on the disc explains, the film was made at the cusp of the CGI revolution and therefore combines accomplished CGI trickery with more traditional live effects and stunning matte shots by Robert Stromberg. Stephen H Burum's imaginative cinematography is combined with the sumptuous and intricate set designs by Joseph Nemec (" a master of layering and technique" according to Burum) to recreate the look of old Hollywood. Burum himself masterminds several tricks of light and shade to realise the battle between good and evil (Cranston's use of the power to cloud men's minds is visualised by shadows obscuring Baldwin's face, for instance, while Margo Lane talks to her father about the effect Cranston has had on her while spider-web patterns play over the ceiling.

The film also features one of the most intricate and inventive scores of Jerry Goldsmith's career. The main theme combines French horns and keyboards with eerie electronic wailing and swooshing to evoke both heroic determination and supernatural stealth. Kahn and his Mongol warriors are backed by Taiko drums, metallic percussion and marching woodwind. Goldsmith's score is dense and layered, driving the story forward and matching the visual glamour of the settings. Among the many stand out scenes is an inspired sequence where an agent of The Shadow delivers a message through the letterbox of the office of B Jonas (from the very first issue, The Living Shadow)and then follows the message as it is hurled through a pneumatic tube, twisting and turning along the side of skyscrapers to the accompaniment of Goldsmith's soaring orchestra until the tube converges with hundreds of others in the lair of Burbank (Andre Gregory)the Shadow's communications operator.

The film's an archness upsets some - Commissioner Barth is played by comedian Jonathan Winters, while Peter Boyle portrays Shrevvy, another agent of The Shadow, with a manic humour- but it is also ingenious. The scene where Cranston admiringly realises the full scope of Kahn's plans and powers, accompanied by Goldmith's elephantine trumpets and some ghostly visuals is a delight. With the knowledge that Orson Welles once played The Shadow on the radio, the climactic battle between Kahn and Cranston evokes the "Hall of Mirrors" sequence out of Welles' "Lady From Shanghai". Even a scene of Cranston walking across a street reveals an intricate matte painting by Robert Stromberg of 1930's Times Square. And the final defeat of Khan is both unexpected and fitting. The fact that "The Shadow" failed to generate a "franchise" should not be held against it. "The Shadow" is a film which repays repeat viewing.

WHEN THE BOAT COMES IN (BBC 1976-1981)

Jack Ford (James Bolam) returns from the First World War to the Tyneside town of Gallowshield. Employment is precarious for shipyard toolfitters like Jack, and miners like the Seaton's - the family Jack becomes involved with after meeting independent schoolteacher Jessie Seaton (Susan Jameson). Jack becomes first a union organiser and then a businessman, determined to improve his lot in life.

Although many boardroom drama's followed *The Plane Makers*, this series, set in depressed Tyneside, created a true heir John Wilder. Both Wilder and Jack Ford are self-made men. True, Jack Ford as played by James Bolam, has a rougher edge than Wilder (a Doctor's son) but Ford proves capable of moving among and besting the gentry. More importantly, both characters have a strategic, calculating nature. The excitement they create comes from seeing all the odds against them at the halfway mark and wondering how they are going to resolve the situation by the end of the show.

"A vote is a weapon that can hit as hard as any hammer, " Jack tells an election crowd, "It's a weapon that some of you are too daft to use!"

When The Boat Comes In was created for the BBC by James Mitchell, until then best known for the ITV spy series *Callan*. Although *When The Boat Comes In* was not a crime/espionage series, the character of Jack Ford (James Bolam) has some similarities with Callan. Both are loners; although Jack Ford has many women, the relationships never last. Both have been psychologically wounded by their experiences - Ford has served as a military interrogator in Murmask.

There are some differences: Where Callan stands apart from society, Jack Ford is entwined with it. Callan is an orphan of war, and Jack Ford's only mention of a family is a comment to Mrs Seaton in the first episode that, "I had a lovely Mam". Unlike Callan he seems to have a need for family relationships. Although he is forced to abandon his sweetheart Jessie Seaton (Susan Jameson) he continues to be involved with her family. In the second series episode, *Whatever Made You Think The War Was Over* , her mother Bella (Jean Garbutt) gets drunk after a family dispute She flirts with Jack ("All my life, just one man. My canny pitman that loved us and needed us. Then you come along.").As she passes out he kisses her, saying, "I Loved You All, Mrs Seaton. I still do." In the final episode, the cynical Scott-Palliser (Clive Merrison) tells Sarah's brother Billy that "You talk about Ford as if he's part of your family". Billy snaps back, "I detest the man," and gets the reply *"Exactly!"*

Just as Callan has a supportive/exploitative relationship with the thief Lonely, Jack Ford has an ambiguous relationship with his friend Matt Headley (Malcolm Terris). But this is more reminiscent of John Wilder and Don Henderson in *The Power Game*. Ford was Matt's sergeant during the war, and Matt hero-worships him. When Jack

Ford is elected as Secretary of the Fitters Union, he appoints Matt as his assistant. When Ford moves into business, he pushes for Matt to take over his job as Secretary and become both a town councillor and Justice of the Peace. Matt undoubtedly benefits from his relationship with Ford, but it is also clear that Jack is using Matt in his commercial ventures. In *Whatever Made You Think The War Was Over*, Jack is unable to act openly against a factory owner and uses Matt's name to make an enquiry with an American union about the safety of machinery that the factory owner has bought. Matt sees the world in clear boundaries, unlike the pragmatic Jack. The only time they fight is when Matt thinks Jack has betrayed his union members in a business deal. It is also Matt's sister Dolly (Madeleine Newton) who Jack gets pregnant - ending his dreams of marrying Jessie Seaton.

Jack's relationship with Matt is mirrored by the recurring characters of Labour MP Geordie Watson (Ian Cullen) and his agent Sid Liddell (Roger Avon). The lugubrious Watson is a pragmatist, who recognises in the second series episode *The Way it Was In Murmansk* that he lacks the fire to win over electors and needs Jack Ford to speak for him at the election. The idealistic Liddell refuses to bargain with Jack, but Watson overrules him. Both characters return in the fourth series - Liddell helps Jack tackle the rise of Fascism in Gallowshields, while Geordie Watson gives Jack inside information which helps increase his fortune. In the episode, *Friends, Romans, Countrymen* both Watson and Liddell are involved in one of the many marches for jobs which preceded the famous Jarrow March. Stan is footsore having walked the 300 miles from Gallowshield while Watson guiltily admits that he was already in London making speeches in Parliament.Later on, Geordie meets Jack at a fundraising party. Jack tries to calm his fears that he's betrayed his class saying, "Only politicians use words like betrayal." Geordie admits that, "I like champagne so I drink it." He adds that, "back home in Gallowshield I drink bitter. I don't like it but I drink it."

The Power Game is also evoked in the series three episodes where Jack leaves the union to become a businessman. In a trilogy written by Colin Morris, Jack is used as a frontman to take over and 'squeeze the assets' of a patriarchal engineering firm run by Ryder (Colin Douglas). The three episodes detail the process by which the confidence of shareholders is undermined in order to tempt them to sell (coincidentally the legal advisor in these episodes is played by Murray Hayne, who played Al Bonner in The Plane Makers episode Sauce For the Goose). Jack's silent partner is Sir Horatio Manners, the father of Jack's commanding officer during the war. The death of Captain Manners is one of Jack's set-pieces throughout the series, a sure-fire seduction technique in which Jack recalls how he held Manners in his arms after a shell burst as he asked, *"What am I doing here, Sergeant. I was supposed to be dining at the Saville."* Sir Horatio has interests in the local shipbuilding firms and becomes both an ally and antagonist of Ford's as Jack moves from being a union representative to a businessman. Sir Horatio is played by Basil Henson, who had been journalist Sandy Warren in both *Front Page Story* and *The Power Game*.

A Land fit for Heroes

The first series of When The Boat Comes in was broadcast from January 1976. It opens in 1919 with Jack Ford (James Bolam) still in uniform as he returns to Gallowshield. Jack is on leave pending discharge after service in Russia. He is chastised by schoolteacher Jessie Seaton (Susan Jameson) for laughing at propaganda films about the recently concluded war. In a pub he explains to Jessie and her brother Tom (John Nightingale) that his laughter was ironic ("it wasn't all brave Tommies and up and at 'em!"). He accepts her invitation to come home ("since you've made up your mind you're one of the family you might as well be on time for supper!"). Jack ingratiates himself with mother Bella (Jean Heywood) and father Bill (James Garbutt) with some bottles whisky and port. With the miners on strike and starving, Jack and his friend Matt Headley steal sheep to feed their families. Principled Jessie objects at first but is soon won over (Tom's wife is dying of consumption and they need the food). Jessie is a socialist who wants to bring about a legal change to the system, but Jack Ford is more interested in direct action. Despite these differences they are passionately in love and seem destined to marry. But in the episode Empire Day at the Slag Heap, Jack learns that he has got Matt's sister pregnant. Jack tells Jessie that he can't marry her, because he has to marry Dolly (Madeleine Newton). At the same time, Bill Seaton's back has been broken in a mining accident. Jack intervenes to get compensation from the Mine Owners.

Bella convinces the wheelchair-bound Bill to invest the compensation money in turning their front room into a shop. Jack secretly builds the shelves they need although Bill tells his family he wants nothing to do with "the fornicating bastard". Meanwhile Jessie marries school headmaster Arthur Ashton. In the episode *King For A Day*, Sir Horatio Manners pays Jack to pose as a businessman so he can negotiate a cut price for a house a member of the impoverished gentry is selling. Ford pulls off his performance at a shooting weekend and learns enough about the motivations of the family to turn the deal to his advantage. Tragically, Dolly loses their child and is told she will never conceive again. In counterpoint, Tom Seaton is left to bring up his young son after his wife dies.In the final episode of the first series (April 1976), Tom Seaton is arrested for theft. Jack breaks into a house to retrieve the furniture of an evicted widow and then waits for the police. He uses his trial to make a speech against inequality. Tom is sentenced to three months in prison, while Jack is sentenced to one month, and returns to a victory parade, elected secretary of the union.

The success of the first series meant that a second series quickly followed in October 1976. As secretary of the Fitters Union, Jack uses his connections with shipyard chairman Sir Horatio Manners to win a pay victory and see off opposition from his hardline rivals. Jessie's brother Billy (Edward Wilson) has graduated from medical school but is unable to get work because of his socialist beliefs. He begins volunteering at the free clinic and comes into conflict with Bill and brother Tom who believe he should get a proper job so he can repay them the money they lent for his medical school fees. Jack continues to socialise with the local gentry, and an out-of-place Dolly leaves him for Tom Seaton.

In the third series, (September 1977) Arthur is offered a housemaster's job at a public school in Kent and Jessie is forced to leave Gallowshield (in real life, Susan Jameson was married to James Bolam and gave birth to their daughter in 1977). While Matt takes over his job at the union, Jack continues to move between the workers and the gentry, introducing a savings stamp scheme to Bill's shops and fronting for Manners to take over a paternalistic but stagnant firm. In the final episode of the series, Jack leaves for America and a career as a bootlegger.

James Bolam spent the next three years starring as the hypochondriac Roy Figgis in Eric Chappel's comedy *Only When I Laugh* for Yorkshire TV. He returned as Jack Ford for the final series in 1981. Where the previous three series had gradually covered a period from 1919 to 1926, the final series cut forward six years to 1930 with Jack having lost his fortune in the Wall Street Crash and returning to England on the run from the mob. This final series concentrated on the now alcoholic Ford trying to rebuild his fortune. On returning to Gallowshield he learns from Sarah Headley (Rosalind Bailey) that Matt has died in a mysterious boating accident. With Tyneside now impoverished and the shipyards closed, Jack sets up a market stall with Sarah and becomes rich once more. Jack unites with the local Labour party to defy Blackshirts in Gallowshield. In London, he meets Billy Seaton – now a wealthy doctor and communist fellow-traveller. Billy and the zealot Scott-Palliser (Clive Merrison) use Jessie (now separated from her husband) to recruit Jack in a scheme to smuggle guns into Spain during the Civil War. Jessie believes the guns will go to the Socialists but Scott-Palliser is under orders from Moscow. Jack will be betrayed to Franco's forces, and the guns will go to the Communists.

When The Boat Comes In is at its strongest in the first three series. Jack Ford's machinations are fascinating to watch, but lent a counterpoint by the characters of the Seaton family. Unlike *The Power Game*, where the Bligh's are often in conflict with John Wilder, the Seaton's are usually the recipients of Jack's good nature. Each character represented a different reaction to the poverty of the 1920's. Idealistic doctor Billy (Edward Wilson)was a hardline socialist, working for barter (usually vegetables or fish) at a free clinic. Billy was unable to get work with the local medical practices because his left-wing views would offend the wealthier patients. Tom (John Nightingale)had scabbed during a strike to feed his dying wife. Later, a widower, Tom is allowed back into the mines only to leave after seeing a 15 year old boy killed during his first day down the pit. Turning to theft, he is jailed but forms a strong friendship with Jack Ford in Durham jail. Released he becomes a gardner, providing Jack's wife Dolly with the simple life Jack can't settle for.

Irascible Bill Seaton (James Garbutt)is a more warm -hearted Caswell Bligh. Crippled in a pit collapse, he is persuaded by Bella to use the compensation won by Jack to open a shop. Initially suspicious, Bill embraces commerce (designing a sign reading 'The Clock Ticks, We Don't') and gradually builds a small empire of shops. Bella (Jean Haywood) prematurely aged by steering the day to day labours of running a pre-electric, pre-welfare state house. Jessie, principled socialist, sometimes self-righteous. After Jack abandons her, she marries her headmaster, Arthur Ashton (Geoffrey Rose, ominously usually credited as 'Ashton' in the closing credits). An effete, upper middle-class Southerner who had moved to Tyneside to be near his first wife's family, Arthur is introduced in the episode *Empire Day at the Slag Heap*, parading the schoolchildren and paying tribute to the glorious dead. With a stiffness to rival Michael Portillo, Arthur is an ambiguous figure, clearly resenting being "second-best" to Jack Ford and coming into conflict with Jessie during the local elections (she puts a 'Labour' poster in the window and he puts a 'Conservative' poster next to it.

Arthur does his best to show affection, doing the books for Bill's shop and swallowing his dislike for Jessie's socialist activities. Probably his finest hour comes in *My Bonny Lass, Goodbye*, where Jessie storms back to her parents house after he tells her he's been offered a job as a housemaster at a public school in Kent. Left alone with their baby son, Arthur finally puts the child in a pram and wheels it through the streets. The sight of a man pushing a pram through the streets (especially in his black coat and bowler hat) draws derision from the children who chase him chanting, "His Daddy is his Mammy". Two women are aghast commenting: She'll have him in a skirt before the bairn's grown. Arthur finally makes it to the Ashton house and wins the family round, explaining that the job brings a guaranteed place for their son at the school, and that he'll be earning more money.

The final series is set apart from the first three both by time and atmopsphere. the storyline concentrates on Jack Ford, passing quickly through the 1930's. We hear a few lines about the Seaton's (sadly John Nightingale had died prematurely the year before) but only meet up again with Jessie and Billy in the final episodes. James Mitchell's scripts are still as sharp as ever, with Jack Ford's social conscience being tested by the rise of fascism, but like the final series of The Power Game, some of the heart has gone out of the show. As with *Callan* , James Mitchell ended the series with Jack Ford betrayed and under fire. Although Ford was able to outwit his enemies, there was no final reprieve for the series.

One interesting little bit of continuity came in James Mitchell's first series February 1976 episode 'Paddy Boyle's Discharge'. Still unemployed Jack is invited to a meeting by former WW1 comrade Sid Hepburn (George Irving) who had served with Jack, Matt and Paddy Boyle. Hepburn and Bartram (Patrick Durkin) are serving in the 'Black and Tans', the para-military force assisting the Royal Irish Constabulary against the Irish Republican Army at a princely ten shillings a day.

While Bartram revels in the job, Hepburn's nerve or conscience is frayed. He wants to get out, and has been promised by a recruiting officer that he'll be released if he can get Jack Ford to sign up. At the station hotel, Jack Ford meets Captain Leslie (Terrence Hardiman) who says Ford's war record showed he worked as an intelligence interrogator in Murmansk. Leslie tries to recruit Ford for the same work in the new Auxiliary Division. "I can get all the thugs and prizefighters I need. I want brains!"

Coincidentally or not, the Callan episode, 'The Worst Soldier I Ever Saw' by James Mitchell featured Ronald Radd as Colonel Leslie. The story had been held over from the first series of Callan in which Radd had played "Hunter", Callan's controller. Radd had been succeeded in the second series by Michael Goodliffe, who was then replaced by Derek Bond. With "Hunter" now established as a codename, the decision was taken to revive the held-over first series episode. New scenes were filmed to show Bond being drafted on a diplomatic mission and Radd's Colonel Leslie agreeing to cover the role of "Hunter". This raises the tantalising question of whether Terrence Hardiman was playing the father of "Hunter" in this episode.

Unfortunately, Hepburn is recognised by Paddy Boyle (Ralph Watson) one of Jack's band of sheep rustlers from earlier in the series. Boyle is a member of the local Irish league and they want the Black and Tans to account for rape and murder in Ireland. Paddy tries to follow Jack to his meeting, but is beaten up by Bartram. Jack stops Bartram from kicking the unconscious Paddy and later visits the Irish lodge to tell him he's refused Captain Leslie's offer.

Later on Jack realises that a drunken Matt has disclosed when the two Black and Tans will be leaving Gallowshield. Boyle had saved the lives of the company (including Hepburn) by throwing a German grenade out of their trench. But as Sid and Bartram wait for their train, Paddy and his leader shoot them down. Jack and Matt run onto the platform just in time to see Captain Leslie open fire. "Mons, Wipers and the Somme," a tearful Matt concludes, "And the poor bugger has to buy it at a bloody railway station."

More recently, When The Boat Come In has returned to its roots. A stage play by Peter Mitchell was performed at the South Shields Custom House in August 2018. Based on James Mitchell's first series scripts, the show was received well enough to justify a sequel in September 2019, When The Boat Comes In: The Hungry Years.

When the Boat Comes In: The Hungry Years by Peter Mitchell, is the second in a projected trilogy based on the 1970's BBC TV series. Premiering at the Customs House, South Shields until September 28th, the play introduces a new generation to the vivid characters and situations created by James Mitchell.

Despite the setting in a depressed 1920's Tyneside, we regard the character of Jack Ford as one of the few true rivals to John Wilder ; a calculating pragmatist who takes the world on his own terms and offers reward to those who follow him. Jamie Brown succeeds in winning over the audience without betraying the ambiguity of the character. His interpretation is distinctly different from the TV original (to coin a phrase, it's as if someone said, "Get me a young George Costigan") but still has the ring of truth.

The play takes aspects of the TV episodes, Paddy Boyle's Discharge, King For A Day, and Kind Hearted Rat With A Lifebelt but Peter Mitchell and director Katy Weir have tightened the strands into a fully theatrical experience. The Jack Ford of the play is much more on edge – whether through conscience or the after-effects of trench warfare – leading to a nightmarish pre-interval explosion. The action takes place against an expressionistic, sliding set that opens in darkness with clanging, grinding noises (shipbuilding or coal hoists?) before the cast gradually appear holding candlelights and singing 'The Internationale' as Jack Ford sorts through the treasures in his kitbox, finally pulling out and spinning the chambers of his service revolver.

The rapid scene changes are turned into an event by having the actors shift the scenery in choreographed moves, sometimes accompanied by contemporary songs. This probably sounds more twee than it actually is . The overall effect keeps the mood of the show consistent and also allows for some shock effects such as (what we've presumed to be) the walls of a house to slide apart to reveal Tom Seaton (Matthew Howden) standing beside the coffin of his wife Mary.

While this is a fresh interpretation, there is also much that remains faithful to the TV show. From the moment Steve Byron yells, "tell that fornicating bastard to go to hell," it's clear that he'll be playing wheelchair-bound Bill Seaton in the irascible manner of James Garbutt. Byron doubles as Ford's mentor, Sir Horatio Manners (played by Basil Henson in the TV show) nailing the upper-class character's foxy charm (sometimes with an extremely quick change). Similarly, Charlie Richmond plays Matt Headley, the straight-as-a-die but hero-worshipping sidekick of Ford like a reincarnation of Malcolm Terris, but also plays Lord Calderbeck, prospective victim of a sting by Manners and Ford.

Anna Bolton makes a sympathetic, three-dimensional Dolly Ford, with some humorous body language and pouting when Jessie Seaton comes to call on Jack. It's Dolly who first alerts Jack to the starving conditions of widow Sarah Balfour (Carrie Downey) and her sons. The plight of the Balfour family, with not enough money coming in to feed the children, is one of those situations which seemed to be part of the dead past in the TV show, and yet now seems frighteningly relevant for the stage show.

The play opens with Jack unemployed due to shipyard layoffs. Sir Horatio Manners offers Jack a chance to make some quick money by posing as a rich businessman at a country house weekend. Later on, union organiser Les Mallow (Adam Donaldson) offers Jack the chance to be his paid assistant if he will use his skills to get Les elected as union secretary.

At the heart of When The Boat Comes In is the tension between Jack's ruthless self-interest, the intellectual socialism of Jessie and union organiser Mallow, and the practical charity of Bella Seaton. Bella is played with great charm by Janine Birkett (who recently appeared as war correspondent Marie Colvin in the drama-documentary Under the Wire). Throughout the play, Bella tries to do what is right, shouting down her opinionated husband or gently coaxing a shattered Jack Ford away from self-pity. Ironically, Alice Stokoe doubles both the principled Jessie and the extremely unprincipled Lady Jessica Croner.

It's great to see these characters live again. The story is entertaining, down-to-earth and salted with wry humour (unexpected bits like the union strike vote where brother Poskett (Luke Maddison) suddenly points at the audience shouting, "You, get your hand up!")

If I had to criticise the play, I'd question why Jack Ford was robbed of his big speech against inequality towards the end. And to see a play about Jack Ford without him trotting out his story about the death of Captain Manners and "Dining at the Saville" seems like Hamlet without "To Be or Not To Be". But those are minor quibbles – and for a play that has the hair standing on the back of my neck more than once, not really relevant.

Youth Is Wasted On The Young

Gerry Anderson's movie Doppelganger was influenced by The Power Game to the extent of casting Patrick Wymark as a 21st Century John Wilder. The next logical move was to follow-up with a movie written by Wilfred Greatorex – script editor of The Plane Makers and The Power Game. Youth Is Wasted On The Young never made it past the script stage but offers a fascinating insight into the route Gerry Anderson's movie career might have taken.

Police outriders flank a Rolls Royce convertible as a convoy speeds down the highway. It sounds like the opening sequence of "Identified" the introductory episode of *UFO* but it's actually the title sequence in the first draft of *Youth Is Wasted On The Young* an original screenplay by Wilfred Greatorex from an idea by Gerry Anderson.

Completed on June 26 1969, the first and only draft identifies the passenger of the Rolls as Marshal Gargano, the 78-year-old dictator of a South American state. The year is 1987, and Gargano speeds to the airport to welcome the Secretary-General of the United Nations as he disembarks from Concorde Mark IX.

In the kitchen-dinette of his home, 38-year-old engineer Paul Cavour eats breakfast as the "wall-TV news" shows Gargano being thanked, "for his work for World Peace." Elly, his "blonde, elegant "32 year old wife cynically heckles the TV as she prepares breakfast for their children.

Cavour travels into the capital city for what he thinks is a business meeting. But when he arrives at the plush office block, his host Renzo tells him that he has passed rigorous vetting to beat 1000 competitors for a job. Cavour is bewildered – he has not applied for a job. His host explains the vetting process, showing him hours of surveillance footage. Cavour having lunch with his secretary, Elly meeting up with her brother (at first, they thought she was having an affair but were relieved to find that the Cavours lead blameless lives).

A proud but worn-down old man is ushered into the office. Renzo asks the old man if they have ever met before. The old man peers at his questioner and says no. The host thrusts a knife into the old man's chest. As Cavour watches the old man crumple to the floor, his host advises that, "there is a case for Euthanasia." He warns Cavour to say nothing.

Cavour returns home, aware that every move is being watched and the safety of his family depends on his compliance. Gradually, he is admitted to the leading social circles and is brainwashed into becoming an acolyte of Gargano, making a televised speech in support of the Marshal which wins fanatical applause. Now a 'poster boy' of the Government, Cavour is driving his own car when he is forced off the road. Cavour is taken to a private hospital, where Gargano's surgeon Ian Wallace goes to work. Surrounded by computers, the surgical team divide their efforts between two operating tables and two patients. "There's a ritual about the operations. They have clearly been rehearsed time and again. There are no histrionics: only work to a plan and a sense of scientific occasion." The operation reaches a climax, as Wallace and his team concentrate on just one patient. The other body is abandoned.

Elly is told that Cavour was dreadfully injured in the car accident, but under Wallace's care he is gradually returned to health. He regains his strength, is named as Gargano's successor and begins indulging in manic recreational activity, playing tennis, swimming, revelling in the strength of his youthful body.

Gradually, Elly realises the truth. Wallace has carried out a brain transplant. She rejects Cavour's advances, telling him *"I'm not your wife. My husband's dead. Mutilated in that abattoir you call a hospital."*

On 4th March 1969, ATV transmitted Wilfred Greatorex's *Power Game* episode, *The Heart Market* . Made less than two years after the WORLD'S first heart transplant had been carried out, it showed one of the leading characters Caswell Bligh (Clifford Evans) felled by a heart attack. With suitable donors of compatible hearts in short supply, the episode explored the way in which men of power and influence could try to jump the queue for new hearts.

Days before *The Heart Market* was transmitted, Gerry Anderson announced that he would be developing Youth Is Wasted On The Young with Wilfred Greatorex. Set once again in the near future of 1987, the screenplay takes the dystopian approach that Greatorex would late explore in the BBC TV series 1990, and blends it with the high-tech effects of Gerry Anderson. Marshal Gargano travels in a luxurious Vertical Take Off and Landing jet which features in several significant scenes. He also employs an automated execution machine which makes firing squads redundant and ensures that enemies of the state can be eliminated on a production-line basis.

The screenplay identifies the capital city as Brasilia, although it is not clear if the film would be set in Brazil (which in 1968 was under military dictatorship) or if Gerry Anderson was just hoping to exploit Oscar Niemeyer's then futuristic designs as a backdrop for an anonymous South American state(perhaps with location filming in Portugal and interiors at Pinewood).

The location in a dictatorship is fundamental to the plot. While the idea of brain transplants wasn't new, either in science fiction or movies, Anderson and Greatorex took a journalistic approach, building on the most recent developments. Heart transplants were incredibly expensive in terms of surgical staff and procedure, and also depended on the exceedingly rare resource of a healthy and compatible heart becoming available. Concerns had already been raised that countries where life was cheap might furnish an unwilling source of raw material. (By coincidence the first episode of ATV's Strange Report (: Report 4407: Heart – No Choice for the Donor) filmed July 1968, but only transmitted January 1970, starred Barbara Murray as the wife of surgeon Robert Hardy, who was being coerced into carrying out a heart transplant on the head of a Mediterranean state, with unwilling donors.)

The transplant of a living brain would have additional costs and complications. Quite apart from the medical complexities, Gargano was actually looking for a young donor body to allow his brain to continue. That would mean to some extent taking on a new identity.

The idea of identity theft had been explored in TV episodes such as *The Outer Limits (The Hundred Days of the Dragon)* and the 1967 movie *The Sorcerors* (where Boris Karloff and Catherine Lacey use a machine to leech the thoughts and feelings of young Ian Ogilvy), but again Anderson and Greatorex were trying something different. Cavour's body is acceptable, but his identity must be gradually changed so that it will be credible when Gargano finally takes possession of his new suit of clothes.

The choice of a futuristic South America as the setting, kills two birds with one stone. It allows for an exotic backdrop attractive to Hollywood finance and provides a credible dystopian setting for a state where bodies can be harvested.

Assuming that Anderson would have pitched the movie to Universal as a follow-up to Doppelganger, it's intriguing to consider who might have starred in the movie. The choice of the name Ian Wallace for Gargano's surgeon makes it tempting to assume that Anderson would have offered the role to Ian Hendry. The role of the conflicted surgeon would have suited Hendry well – especially when he has to confront Gargano's henchmen after they eliminate the rest of the surgical team following the successful operation. As for the South American dictator, it's possible that Anderson might have wanted to retain the Power Game connection by casting Clifford Evans.

Cavour is described as being "handsome in a Roman way", which leaves the role open for any number of American leading men. However, if Universal had financed the project Tony Franciosa from Universal's TV series The Name of The Game might have lent depth to the role. The actor playing Cavour would need to depict his early paranoia has he returns home realising that every room in his house is bugged. He would have to develop into brainwashed enthusiasm and then change gear to portray Gargano within Cavour's body. Although Greatorex writes Gargano as ruthless, he allows him a moment of sympathy, admitting that, "I sign death warrants, but a lot more died before I took over."

As for Elly Cavour, this is a particularly strong female role. The storyline has elements of gothic horror (or outre movies *like The Alligator People and I Married A Monster From Outer Space*) as Elly becomes disturbed by the change in her husband and horrified by the realisation that the mind inside his body belongs to someone else. Her role gradually expands as she tries to find an escape route for her children. There were any number of talented young British or American actresses who could have played the role. But let's be realistic, this was the British Film Industry circa 1969 and the role would probably have ended up going to some poor European actress dubbed by Nikki van der Zyl.

The final major character in the movie is Pieter Valde. He is a principled army officer, who attempts to oppose Gargano but has to go underground after 23 of his fellow officers are massacred. He provides a potential escape route for Elly and again it's tempting to think that Gerry Anderson would have preserved the *Power Game Doppelganger* link by casting George Sewell in the role. Of course, much would have depended on whoever got appointed to the director's chair.

Gerry Anderson was already filming the first episode of UFO when Wilfred Greatorex completed this draft. The project is said to have failed because of script problems. It's difficult to say just what those problems were. It's possible that the storyline was considered to be a bit of a downer. But then perhaps no more than films that did get made like Beneath The Planet of the Apes, Soylent Green and The Omega Man.

It's arguable that a studio may have thought *Youth* difficult to sell – is it science fiction, is it a totalitarian thriller, is it a horror movie? In truth it has aspects of all three – in some ways it's a David Cronenberg movie ahead of its time. With so much of Gerry Anderson's back catalogue being resurrected, perhaps the time will come when the screenplay is revived and YOUTH is no longer wasted.

thanks to Victoria Bennett of the British Film Institute Special Collections for her help in viewing Wilfred Greatorex's screenplay.

The Investigator

"The Man Who Felt Branson's Collar" would have been an apt title for the autobiography of Michael Knox, the Customs investigator who arrested Richard Branson in 1971 for purchase tax fraud. But Knox's experiences are far wider than this isolated incident, dealing with fuel fraud, preventing the import of drugs and pornography and eventually helping to negotiate the single market structure which, he ruefully observes, is about to be undone by the Brexit vote.

Michael Knox was an officer in the Investigations Branch of HM Customs and Excise, the organisation which merged with the Inland Revenue in 2005 to create the current HM Revenue & Customs.Just saying that clues you in to the historic scope of this book. Knox joined the Investigation Branch in 1968. He was inspired to apply to the Branch by *The Revenue Men*, a 1967 BBC2 TV series starring Ewen Solon as Caesar Smith, an Investigation Branch officer based in Scotland. Knox retired in 1996 shortly after the premiere of *The Knock*, ITV's series about a Collection Investigation Unit in London. If you can't remember *The Knock*, you'll realise just how long ago this book is set. But it is an important book. Ground level customs investigation work has been detailed in Jon Frost's cheery *Anything To Declare?* (2015) and Harry Ferguson's *Lima 3* (2005) which related the stresses of tackling organised drug gangs. But the scope of Knox's career was much wider, being involved with the Arms to Iraq case and providing much of the detail in the system that was to form Britain's contribution to the Single Market.

While the Branson case has been well documented, Knox implies that inaccuracies crept into previous accounts. Purchase Tax was the predecessor of VAT, introduced by the British Government in 1940 and putting a 33 and a third percent charge on luxury goods such as records. When Richard Branson was getting Virgin Records off the ground he realised that he could evade Purchase Tax by claiming to have exported the records to France and then turning back once he'd got his export documents stamped at Dover. After a tip from a disgruntled competitor, Knox realised that the discount Virgin was selling records for would have eroded any profit margin if they were actually paying tax.

Knox acknowledges the tensions between the IB and the Purchase Tax control officers who viewed the IB as "glory boys..leaving the mess to be sorted out after they'd trampled all over some poor officer's...relationships with traders that had been carefully nurtured over years." He amusingly recalls the careful negotiations he had to make with his own colleagues to gain an audience with the young Branson. Once he had gained access to Virgin's paperwork, Knox became sure there was fraud, and set up an elaborate sting to prove that the records covered by the export documents had been diverted for sale in mainland Britain. Knox writes engagingly about the progress of the case and clearly has some admiration for Branson (on the drive down to Dover Police Station for the formal charge, Knox decided they should stop off at a pub, "no handcuffs..just a quiet drink and a friendly chat"). He notes that Branson's night in the cells made him resolve never again to succumb to a temptation that might result in losing his liberty.

The scope of *The Investigator* reminds me in a way of James Stewart in *The FBI Story*, with each chapter covering a different stage in the progression of his career. Before joining the IB, Knox was appointed to one of the first Road Fuel Testing Units, searching for truck drivers running illegally on duty-relieved Red Diesel. After a fruitless month taking random samples of fuel, Knox decided to improvise and began asking the police constable in each area they visited to name the local dodgy characters. Armed with this intelligence, Knox soon increased his rate of detection. Following this success, he was admitted to the Investigation Branch where he began hunting for haute couture dresses being smuggled in from Paris to avoid both import duty and purchase tax, new jewellery passed off as second-hand (again to avoid tax) and cannabis smugglers.

At times it's necessary to remind yourself of historical conditions. Knox recalls the exchange controls which had been in force since 1930's, limiting the amount of cash that could be taken abroad to Twenty Five Pounds (and later Fifty Pounds) . In the 1957 movie *The Birthday Present*, when toy salesman Tony Britton is caught trying to smuggle an expensive watch into London Airport, one of the questions the customs officers are interested to ask is how Britton found the money to buy the watch. As Knox comments, "most of us couldn't afford what was regarded as a meagre allowance." Similarly, Knox has to remind us of the distinction between 'soft pornography' sold in Soho bookshops ("plenty of nipples but not a public hair insight") and the harder porn imports. Whereas police officers had to prove that pornography was liable to "deprave or corrupt" Customs officers only had to prove that an item was "obscene" (and in 1971 pubic hair was obscene).Still a subjective opinion, but easier to prove in court. One of the raids on a Soho bookshop related in the book verges on the farcical and calls to mind Adam Faith and Iain Cuthbertson in the TV series *Budgie*

In the 1980's, Knox moved from investigation to negotiation. He joined International Customs at HQ, working to build the European Community Customs Code. This brought together all the regulations to control borders in a single document. The aim was to ensure that importers and exporters in each EU member state were subject to the same rules. In practice, agreement with all the member states was difficult. On a number of occassions, "we had to drop the imperative word 'will' and agree instead to 'member states *may*.. to allow a degree of choice as to whether a particular article had to be applied or not." Knox admits that he was often stubborn in these negotiations because the UK "was always punctilious in applying the legislation. Whereas a number of other member states...only applied them in the breach, effectively only paying lip service to the requirements." *In this sentence Knox gives a clue to why the British have always had problems with working in Europe. We treat the regulations as if it was sheet music to be followed in a stately march, where other member states prefer to take a jazz approach, with the regulations being a tune around which they will improvise.* Nevertheless, Knox persevered and, until the Community Customs

Code was replaced by the Union Customs Code in 2016, his work provided the bedrock for intra-community movements.

Then in 1987, Margaret Thatcher astounded everyone by signing up to the Single European Act which paved the way to freedom of movement and the end of internal borders. Knox was given "three weeks to come up with a comprehensive plan to prepare for the removal of frontiers by 1 January 1993." His high-level strategy for the next six years was accepted by the many interested parties (not just tax, but security, patents, food controls) and he was then tasked with defining the fine-detail. This entailed a trip around Europe observing the baroque procedures and delays involved in controlling and verifying movements. Some of his observations are fascinating, underlining the effort and imagination which was required to ensure freedom of movement across borders. *It would no doubt make informative reading for the Brexiteers who will be charged with finding a "technological" solution to the task of re-building those borders.*

Just over the Brenner Pass on the Austro-Italian border, he came across hundreds of trucks parked around a newly built administration building. *"If you can't change the rules, change the infrastructure...(the Italians)...were marvellous engineers but hopeless administators."* To lodge their declarations, driver had to hand in the main customs document at one window, then walk down to another window to hand in supporting documents, and a third window to hand in health certificates etc. *"if he was lucky his clearance papers would be ready in three hours."*

Europe found a precursor to the Single Market in the Schengen Convention, which kept traffic flowing on the cross-border motorways by allowing residents of the EU states to cross borders without checks. In the run-up to the Single Market, Knox (along with Doug Tweddle, who was in charge of the CHIEF Customs computer system) proposed a simplification of UK Customs import checks. *"it allowed importers to submit their entries or declarations ahead of their arrival in the country...(they) could then be cleared as soon as they landed...this would reduce waiting times by hours."*

However, it became clear that politically, the UK would not give up, *"our island advantage for certain prohibitions and restrictions without a fight."* Over the months, Knox worked with the Treasury and HMCE to put forward a proposal in which the UK could still collect VAT and Excise duties without border checks.Finally, a meeting was arranged with Chancellor Norman Lamont. *"He opened the meeting, looking down at my paper which had been placed before his arrival on the table in front of him and exclaimed, "Is this the paper I haven't read?* Luckily, most of the proposals for free movement were eventually agreed by the EU. From the perspective of 2016, just after the Bexit vote, Knox suggests it will mean *"a weaker trade deal...and the return of border tariffs with the necessary submission of Customs declarations and frontier delays. If this were to happens, I only hope they remember the success of my Fast Lane in the three years leading up to 1993. I really should have patented it.*

As noted at the start, this is a work of history. After HM Customs and Excise merged with the Inland Revenue to form HM Revenue and Customs, much of the "protection of society work" was hived off to the newly created Serious Organised Crime Agency and UK Border Force. The book will tell you little about current anti-smuggling procedures, but does provide a valuable insight into the way society worked in the last half of the 20th Century. It is a competent and entertaining read.   **The Investigator: Drugs, Guns, Gems and Porn - Inside the Secretive World of Customs Investigation**

Michael Knox Milo Books Ltd 2016 ISBN 978-1-908479-89-1

Reckless Opportunists

With each astounding new moment of farce and larceny in British politics, the one essential guide is Aeron Davis' Reckless Opportunists: Elites at the end of the Establishment.   Written after 20 years of talking to individuals in power, it seeks to explain our new generation of leaders, "plugged into power, money or both: someone who knows where their interests lie." But not really in charge. Neither expert nor visionary, nor really in control. "Too many are just reckless opportunists making the best of what they have amid the chaos they have helped create."

Davis explores the way in which neoliberalism, preaching a smaller state, poorer employees, and untaxed capital, has undermined the Establishment which relies on security, law and social stability. Both Blair and Cameron refashioned their parties as "election winners rather than representative parties," leading to a fall in membership and the 2016 election in which the political elite, "were given a good kicking."

At the same time, ambitious civil servants learned the only path to advancement was cutting their own departments and company directors came under pressure from investors to take decisions which would create short term gain and long term pain.

According to Davis, politicians with expertise or experience of the outside world have gradually been replaced by PPE graduates, most of whom work in think-tanks or other political organisations before standing for Parliament. Once elected, the ambitious MP is moved from post-to-post relying on briefs from Civil Servants and party advisors to plug the gaps. The same principle applies to company executives and journalists. "Being a leader means subcontracting out judgement to others who may, or may not, have hidden agenda. It means confidently speaking lines that others have written for you."

Cynics will take comfort in the chapter exploring public consultations, which quotes a former permanent secretary saying, "..many a consultation has already decided the outcome by the time you get to the formal public stage."   The same chapter observes that, "in public, elites of all kinds refer to economist opinions as almost scientific facts. But in private, personal experience shows that too much of economics is too abstract for personal application. "Yet despite this, everyone sticks to the party line. Davis quotes the story of Tony Dye, one of the few fund managers who saw through the dot-com boom but spoke too soon. "Those people who had done the wrong thing – in finance – in politics – had not only survived, they had flourished."   Davis concludes that the people who run our Government, Business and Finances may be highly educated, but they are far less in control than we think. "They follow more than they lead."   Davis ends by suggesting "Systems and Principles for reigning in the Elite" in order to produce more appropriate leaders. Although, as he says elsewhere, turkey's rarely vote for Christmas.

Reckless Opportunists by Aeron Davis – £9.99 Manchester University Press

The Bitter Harvest of Patrick Hamilton

BITTER HARVEST (1963)

TWENTY THOUSAND STREETS UNDER THE SKY (2005)

BITTER HARVEST (1963) stars Janet Munro and John Stride in a compromised adaptation of Patrick Hamilton's trilogy *Twenty Thousand Streets Under The Sky*. Munro played Jenny, a girl from the back streets of Wales whose taste for luxury ultimately destroys her. Stride played the idealistic barman in love with her. Updated to the 1960's and undermined by behind-the-scenes disputes the film was not a success, and it would be another 40 years before the BBC could present a more faithful TV adaptation of Hamilton's work. Ironically, both adaptations were scripted by high profile writers - Ted Willis and Kevin Elyot.

Patrick Hamilton is today probably best-known for the filming of his stage plays *Gaslight*(1940) and *Rope* (1948). When his eve-of-war novel *Hangover Square* was filmed in 1945, it was reimagined as a Victorian gothic to make it more of a piece with *Gaslight*. But before his Hollywood success, Hamilton had been the acclaimed author of contemporary novels which dealt with the underside of London life. Published in 1929, when Hamilton was only 25, *The Midnight Bell* told the story of Bob, a pub barman who falls in love with Jenny, a prostitute. Desperate to stop her selling herself to other men, he depletes his savings in order to loan her money that is never repaid. The story had its roots in Hamilton's own hopeless love for a sex worker, informing the satirical detail of Bob's humiliation. Hamilton was a determined drinker by this stage, and shows Bob after a final betrayal by Jenny, *"surrender (ing) to the explicit demands of drama...deliberately attempting to get wildly drunk and do mad things."*.

Following the success of the novel, Hamilton married Lois Martin who managed to limit his drinking while he wrote the second book in the trilogy. *The Siege Of Pleasure* told Jenny's story - how she won a job as a domestic servant, but was seduced on a drunken night out and had no alternative but a life of prostitution. While Hamilton was writing the novel, he was hit by a car while walking in Earls Court with his wife and sister. Hamilton was dragged through the streets, resulting in injury and disfigurement. Hamilton incorporated the life-changing accident into the novel, with Jenny's drunken night out ending in a hit-and-run. Although she did not drive the car, Jenny shares in the guilt and it forms part of her decision to abandon her respectable life as a wage slave.

In 1934, Hamilton published the final novel in the trilogy *The Plains of Cement*. This runs in parallel with *The Midnight Bell* but tells the story of barmaid Ella, who is in love with Bob, but who he only regards as a friend. Ella is pursued by Eccles, a middle-aged customer who thinks of himself as a 'character' but who is really only irritating. Despite his self-centredness, Eccles represents a prospect of escape for Ella.

Hamilton continued to write into the 1950's, with two plays performed on the BBC Home Service (Radio 4) and more novels including 'Mr Stimpson and Mr Gorse (later televised as *The Charmer*). He died in September 1962, while *Bitter Harvest* was in production. It's clear that the producers wanted to have their cake and eat it - winning the coveted 'X Certificate' for (what now seems tame) sexual content while minimising the screen time Jenny spends as a prostitute. Reversing what had happened with the film of *Hangover Square* Ted Willis' script updated the story from 1929 to 1962. The structure of the three novels was simplified (the producers of the 2005 TV version observed that Hamilton's overlapping timescales have more in common with films like *Pulp Fiction*). Willis took Jenny's background story from *The Siege of Pleasure* but moved the location from a London suburb to an impoverished pit village 30 miles away from Cardiff, everyone having moved away after the pit closed. Perhaps this was done to give Jenny a starting point that was closer to the limited opportunities of the 1930's rather than the fuller employment of the 1960's. Hamilton had shown Jenny winning and doing a good job as a domestic servant to elderly sisters. Willis changes the sisters to Jenny's aunts. The prospect of "taking care of them" as unpaid help is presented as a threat to Jenny who aspires to something better.

The film has an extended sequence showing Jenny watching a TV soap advert that promises a celebrity lifestyle. The *Rose Petal* adverts are referenced two or three times throughout the movie. At one point Jenny recalls watching the adverts, *"People had such fabulous things..then you switch off and you're back in the village...why do they show us these things if we're not meant to have them?"* The implication appears to be that Jenny is seduced by the commercialisation of TV. For Willis, a writer of social conscience, a former Young Communist and later Labour party Peer, it may have been a natural link to make. Ironically, Peter Cotes recalled producer Julian Wintle of being dismissive of "message movies" but the corrupting influence of TV was a popular theme at the time for the film distributors who were being hit hard by competition from TV. In Hamilton's books, of course, it is the movie makers who present the unrealistic dreams (The real-life inspiration for Jenny is said to have resembled silent film star Esther Ralston, one of Hamilton's favourites (In *The Case of Lena Smith* (1929) she played a seduced and exploited country girl).

Somewhat improbably, Jenny is tempted to make use of her employers' ensuite bathroom and is discovered in the bath when leering husband William Lucas comes home early from a business trip. For the first time Jenny becomes aware that she has something to trade, as Lucas gives her five pounds to buy a negligee and come back to 'model it' for him. Although Jenny hands back the money when she realises the implication, the scene shows her realising that she may have a way out of her hopeless situation. As in the book, Jenny meets a salesman (Terence Alexander) who escorts her on a drunken night out - and she wakes up in the bed of one of his friends in London! Whereas in the book, Jenny is socially cut off from her past, in the movie she is geographically far from home.

The script then moves to an approximation of *The Midnight Bell* as Bob notices Jenny in the pub where he works. But where Jenny is already a prostitute in the novel, she is just an abandoned innocent at this stage of the movie. This was John Stride's first substantial film role, although he had achieved stage success playing Romeo opposite Judi Dench (and later Joanna Dunham) in Franco Zefferelli's Old Vic production of *Romeo and Juliet*, and had raised his New York profile as Duncan in *Macbeth* (he would play Ross in Polanski's later film version). Both Peter Graham Scott and Peter Cotes would later disown the casting of this movie - Scott obviously picking up the movie after filming had begun, and Cotes stating that Wintle cast actors who always played the same types, whereas Cotes preferred to use personal knowledge of actors from the stage. Cotes gives an example of Wintle wanting to cast Herbert Lom in the role eventually played by Alan Badel. It seems likely then, that Cotes had lobbied for Stride based on his stage success as Romeo. With the basis of hindsight, and his fiery lead role in *The Main Chance*, he does seem a surprising choice as the guileless Bob.

Ella, the third side of the triangle, is played by Anne Cunningham, one of the original cast of *Coronation Street* (1960 - ad nauseum) as Elsie Tanner's daughter Linda Cheveski for the first year of the show. Ella's role is incredibly truncated (when you consider that Hamilton gave her a whole novel) and the role of her admirer, Mr Eccles is correspondingly brief. Eccles is played here by Allan Cuthbertson, an example of the perfectly competent but assembly-line casting of the movie (Norman Bird as the Guvnor, Vanda Godsell as his wife, Colin Gordon as a bit part actor). One of the high spots of the movie is the set design by Alex Vetchinsky (*North West Frontier, A Night To Remember*) which captures a point in time when Victorian Britain overlapped with the post-war Welfare State. The cluttered shelves of the corner shop in Wales, the exfoliative wallpaper in Bob's apartment house and the interior of the pub itself convey an understated attention to detail. While it has been suggested that Hamilton's model for the pub was *The Prince of Wales Feathers* on Warren Street, the movie exteriors were filmed at the now demolished *King and Queen* in Harrow Road.

Bob offers to let Jenny stay at his bedsit. Unlike the Bob of the novel, although he offers to remain chaste (sleeping in a chair), he is eventually offered the chance to share the bed with Jenny (one of the big X Certificate moments). Although he doesn't give Jenny money for her rent (as in the novel), Bob still finds his savings being depleted as his landlady tells him she charges more rent for two! The scene of Bob discussing his rent in Mrs Jessup's bedroom as she eats her cornflakes is one of the best in the movie. It's another of the film's mysteries as to why Thora Hird, 20 years into her career and recently second billed *A Kind Of Loving* (1962) isn't even credited here . Ironically, despite a line about her late husband being fond of his bed, the scene would have been filmed before the BBC *Comedy Playhouse* - 'The Bed' (December 1963) which led to Thora's long running sitcom with Freddie Frinton, *Meet The Wife*.

At first Bob and Jenny behave like newlyweds in a comedy, with Laurie Johnson's score upbeat and lively. But then, Jenny is invited to a showbiz party where she thinks she might be able to further her 'career' as a model. Drunk once more, she catches the eye of Alan Badel - already starring in Wintle's *This Sporting Life* (1963) and soon to co-star in <u>*Children Of The Damned*</u> . Badel, as if aware that the film is running out of time, summons Jenny to a party the next evening. Drunk and jealous,

Bob crashes the party and pleads with Jenny to come away with him. But she cruelly rejects him - he can't give her what she wants. Which is luxury. As Bob leaves, Badel outlines the future for Jenny - a nice little Mews flat and the rack of clothes she'd dreamed about while watching TV adverts. But since this is a flashback, we know these luxuries will be a *Bitter Harvest*.

The background to *Bitter Harvest* is an epic in its own right*. In early 1962, *Twenty Thousand Streets Under The Sky* was announced as due to be produced for Rank distributors by Leslie Parkyn and Julian Wintle of Independent Artists at their Beaconsfield Studios. The adaptation was written by Ted Willis, then seven years into writing the BBC's *Dixon of Dock Green*. The original director was Peter Cotes, head of drama at Rediffusion TV. Cotes had previously been contracted by Associated British Pictures to direct the film version of Willis' TV play *The Young and The Guilty* (1958) and had cast **Janet Munro** in the featured role of a misunderstood teenager.

Although a critical success, the film had been released a year later as the bottom half of a double bill with *Alive And Kicking*. By then, Janet Munro had been offered a contract by Walt Disney (*Darby O'Gill And The Little People Swiss Family Robinson*). Her management limited the Disney contract to one film a year, so that she would be free to take up offers in the UK and by 1963, Independent Artists was eager to cast her in the star role of *Bitter Harvest*. Munro had already accepted adult roles such as *Girl In A Bird Cage* (ABC 1962)in which she played a girl jailed for wounding her lover, and she had also filmed a bathroom scene calculated to raise temperatures in *The Day The Earth caught Fire* .

Peter Cotes' relationship with Julian Wintle deteriorated during pre-production as it became clear that the producers required a more sensationalistic approach. After two weeks of filming, Cotes was fired by Wintle, stating that his footage was uncommercial. Cotes was replaced by Peter Graham Scott who had been contracted to direct an episode of *The Human Jungle*). Scott, who had recently directed Independent Artists' *The Cracksman* starring Charlie Drake, was clearly their idea of a more commercial director.

But it was an awkward situation for both men since Scott had worked under Cotes at Rediffusion. But Scott was under contract, and as Cotes subsequently discovered when he sued Independent Artists for unfair dismissal, the contracts were legally feudal, with a clear master-servant relationship. When the case was heard at the High Court in 1968, the Judge, Mr Justice McKenna ruled that the company had not acted unfairly because the producers, *"sincerely believed (Cote's) version of the film would fail.*"*. However, although he was ordered to pay costs, Peter Cotes felt he was morally vindicated. The judge had noted that *Bitter Harvest* had lost Â£140,000. Having viewed the finished movie and compared it with Cotes' rushes, he concluded that, *"I cannot imagine a good or successful film being made of this script by Mr Cotes or anybody else."* However, he concluded that, *"I think that Mr Cotes' film would have been more pleasing to the public than the finished film."*

Cotes never directed a film again, believing he had been 'blacklisted' for taking legal action against independent Artists. However, he did go on to direct TV plays for Anglia Television and also mounted his own stage productions. These included Lesley Storm's *Look No Hands* at the Fortune Theatre in July 1971, which was Janet Munro's last stage performance before her death in 1972 (You can read more about Janet Munro in the biography of her husband Ian Hendry. While the failure of the film appears to have killed John Stride's chances as a leading man in movies, he had won the lead in the BBC's adaptation of *The Scarlet And The Black* by May 1965, joined the National Theatre, and following his role in *The Main Chance* was voted top male actor of 1970 by readers of the *TV Times*.

With the movie disowned as a suitably bitter experience by the makers, *Twenty Thousand Streets Under the Sky* was finally dramatised by Frederick Bradnum for BBC Radio 4 in 1989 with Steven Pacey (*Blakes Seven*) as Bob, Annette Badland (*Midsomer Murders*) as Ella, Emily Morgan (*Brass*) as Jenny and John Moffatt (radio's Hercule Poirot) as Ernest Eccles.

In 2005, BBC 4 commissioned a new adaptation of *Twenty Thousand Streets Under the Sky*. Initially broadcast over three nights in April 2005, followed by a two and a half hour complilation on Saturday 23 April, the serial was repeated on BBC 2 over three Fridays in September 2005. The script was by Kevin Elyot, whose 1994 stage play, *My Night with Reg* had been an award-winning success. His 1990 BBC play *Killing Time*, starring Pip Donaghy as a Dennis Nilson figure had also won a Writers Guild award. For the rest of this sadly short career, he balanced more personal projects with ITV Agatha Christie screenplays such as *Curtain:Poirot's Last Case* and *Marple: The Mirror Crack'd From Side To Side*. The adaptation of **Twenty Thousand Streets Under the Sky** was done on a very low budget, meaning the story had to be 'closed down'.

Many exterior scenes in the book were relocated to the small number of sets constructed for the TV show. In some ways, this intensified the sense of claustrophobic authenticity. Ironically (given Elyot's later career) the production team avoided the art deco look of *Poirot*, setting the characters in more run-down faded-Victorian surroundings.

They also took the decision to reinstate the overlapping time periods of the original. Faced with a small cast and a limited number of extras, director Simon Curtis (*My Week with Marilyn*) was struck by Bill Brandt's 1930's photographs, isolating solitary characters against stark backgrounds. According to the DVD commentary he originally thought of filming the series in black-and-white, but eventually compromised with desaturated colours which create an appropriate mood of coal and tobacco mistiness. On the DVD commentary, producer Kate Harwood notes that the costume designer realised that they would have to use patterns rather than colours to differentiate the costumes, contributing to the authentic period atmosphere. The costumes worn by the characters often clash because working class people in the

1930's could only afford a few clothes and chose combinations on the basis of how warm they were, rather than whether they matched.

The four leads were captivating. Bryan Dick (later Ernie Wise in the 2011 Morecambe and Wise bioplay *Eric and Ernie*) presents Bob's essential good nature and contrasting dreaminess (*"the hysteria and obsession of his pursuit"*. Zoe Tapper (*Survivors 2008*) is a subtly unpredictable Jenny - selfish, deceitful, but with enough humanity to make Bob's love for her believable. Sally Hawkins (*Paddington, Godzilla*) is heartbreaking as Ella, silently in love with Bob, her story now restored to its full length in the final episode. We see the home life she has escaped, her mother (Susan Wooldridge) trapped in an abusive marriage. We see the vague prospect of escape being held out to her as Nanny to the children of a middles class family emigrating to India. In *Bitter Harvest* Ella's suitor had been reduced to a couple of lines from regular support actor Allan Cuthbertson. In the TV show, the incomprehensible Ernest Eccles is given his full due played by Philip Davis (*Quadrophenia, Brighton Rock*).

Davis had recently worked with Sally Hawkins in *Vera Drake* (2004) (and would work again with Zoe Tapper in *The Curse of Steptoe* (2008) in which he played Wilfred Brambell and she played Sheila Steafel). Davis manages to make Eccles both grotesque and slightly pathetic. Is it worse being pursued by Eccles or *being* Eccles? Is Eccles, Patrick Hamilton's vision of what he would become if he did not pull himself away from the pubs of Fitzrovia?

The BBC adaptation of *Twenty Thousand Streets In the Sky* unravels, and reinstates the characters and situations crumpled together in *Bitter Harvest*. Its humanity could come as a surprise to those viewers who think they know what to expect from the later, more embittered Patrick Hamilton, and stands as a fitting adaptation of the work of, a writer who is constantly in danger of being forgotten.

Peter Cotes' comments on the background to **Bitter Harvest can be found in a 1990 interview for the British Entertainment History Project (historyproject.org.uk). The outcome of his legal action and comments by the Judge were reported in the Daily Mirror 27 November 1968.*

SPYSHIP (1983)

"I want to know a secret. And everyone is determined to keep me from it." Martin
Taylor (Tom Wilkinson)

**1983: In the sea between Russia and Norway, as the forces of NATO and the
Soviet Union keep a wary eye on each other, the British Fishing
Vessel *Caistor* disappears in mysterious circumstances....**

**Broadcast in November 1983, *SPYSHIP* was a 6-part TV serial, adapted
by *Callan* creator James Mitchell from the 1981 novel by TV journalists Tom
Keene and Brian Haynes. The novel was inspired by their ITV *This
Week* documentaries investigating the 1974 disappearance of the Hull
trawler *Gaul*. This review considers the TV show and the events which inspired
it.**

**A BBC co-production with Australia's 7 Network and America's Arts and
Entertainment,** *Spyship* was produced at BBC Birmingham by Colin Rogers. A
former ATV producer (*A Bunch of Fives* (1977) starring Lesley Manville), Rogers
moved to BBC Birmingham, where he would later produce the 1992 BBC adaptation
of John Harvey's novels about the Nottingham detective *Resnick* (again starring Tom
Wilkinson). *Spyship* was directed by Michael Custance, who had previously directed
episodes of ATV shows such as *The Feathered Serpent* (1976) and Philip Martin's
apocalyptic BBC2 play *The Unborn* (1980).

The night before it sails from Hull, *the British trawler* **Caistor** *is fitted with special
equipment under the supervision of Harding (Malcolm Tierney), who has chartered
the vessel. The next morning, Johnno (Joe Belcher), the chief engineer on
the* **Caistor** *is accompanied to the docks by his son, journalist Martin Taylor (Tom
Wilkinson). Martin has been visiting, following his mother's funeral, and Johnno has
tried to encourage Martin to take up with his old schoolfriend Suzy (Lesley
Nightingale), who is now divorced. Suzy brings Johnno a fruit cake. He jokingly says
it's unlucky for women to come and see the ship off, but hugs her farewell.*

In London, Irving (George Baker) *tells Sir Peter Hilmore (Michael Aldridge) that
Russian subs will be testing new equipment in the middle of NATO exercises, and
asks if the* **Caistor** *can be moved outside its normal fishing grounds for 12 hours to
carry out listening operations. Hilmore agrees, but during a storm, the* **Caistor** *is hit
by a massive force and begins to flood. After a search, the ship is assumed lost with
all hands. In London, Hilmore asks Francis Main (Peter Eyre) to* **"see there's no
evidence left which might be embarrassing to either side."**. *Main has clandestine
meetings with Rokoff (David Burke), his Soviet opposite number and also controls
Evans (Philip Hynd), an ascetic 'dirty tricks' operative. When the brother of
a* **Caistor** *crewman (Malcolm Hebden) raises money to organise a search for
wreckage, Main frames him for theft of the funds. Rokoff arranges for a life buoy,*

*supposedly from the **Caistor** to be found off the coast of Norway. Admiralty scientist Dowdall (Thorley Walters) deduces that the buoy has never been in deep water and Main's assistant Simon (Paul Geoffrey) rewrites the report to remove this conclusion.*

*During the Board of Trade enquiry into the loss of the **Caistor**, relatives protest that the Russians have got their men, and the rumour that the ship was on a spy mission gets into the national press. Harding (Malcolm Tierney) tells Main that the widow of the ships wireless operator received a letter mentioning the new equipment. Main sends Evans to destroy the letter but he kills the wireless operator's widow when she discovers him searching the house.*

The local Labour MP asks a question in Parliament about Russian involvement, and Hilmore tells Main to make sure there is no evidence to contradict the Prime Ministers' statement that the Russians were not involved. Martin has realised that a photo he took of his father's departure shows the extra equipment on the Caistor's mast. Evans finds Martin's notes in Suzy's flat and pressures Main into letting him "retire" Martin, letting Main know that he's been taping all their phone conversations. Hilmore discovers that Evans killed the wireless operator's widow. He gives Main the option of facing a board of inquiry or resigning, and tells Simon to take over the operation, saying that Main has given his operatives, "a purchase over all of us.".

Through her job at the university, Suzy puts Dowdall in contact with Martin (who has survived Evans' attempt to 'retire' him). Dowdall tells Martin that his suppressed report into the buoy indicated that it had never been in deep water and had been planted on the Norwegian coast. While Martin investigates the discovery of the buoy in Norway, Dowdall uses his "old school tie" to call upon Sir Philip Stang (David Ryall), who happens to be Hilmore's superior. Suzy is attacked by Evans to find out where Martin is. In Norway, Evans makes another attempt to kill Martin but it's Evans who ends up dead.

*Returning to England, Martin tricks his way into the psychiatric hospital where Captain Huninger (Michael Lees), who was leading the Royal Navy search for the **Caistor**, is being treated for a breakdown. Martin learns the truth about the **Caistor**, but is captured by Hilmore's men. Hilmore appeals to Martin to suppress the truth, telling him that his activity has ensured thirty years of peace in the west. Hilmore releases Martin but is then confronted by Strang. Rokoff has told Moscow that Hilmore had a KGB man killed in Glasgow and both Main and Simon have told Strang that Hilmore masterminded the 'dirty tricks' operations. With Hilmore sidelined, Simon takes over Main's regular strolls with Rokoff, as Main listens to their conversation over a radio.*

72

As a conspiracy thriller, *Spyship* is an oddity because the central situation so closely resembled something that had happened in recent memory. Although the writers of the novel said that it was not about the *Gaul*, there are a number of similarities, as you can see below. The notion that the crew of the trawler had been captured by the Russians may seem fanciful in hindsight, but at the time there were still fresh memories of the 'Cod Wars', where trawlers and crews had been taken into custody by the Icelandic navy - a friendly power. So it was not much of a stretch to imagine that the nuclear bogieman of the Soviet Union was behind the disappearance of a trawler. Nevertheless, this notion had already been discounted by the TV documentaries and Keene and Hayne's novel, and the TV serial makes it clear that the vessel has sunk, although the cause is still a mystery.

The adaptation is credited to James Mitchell, the creator of *Callan* and *When The Boat Comes In*, but additional scenes are credited to Robert Smith, who would write several plays and TV episodes in the 1980's and 90's including an original screenplay about the Julia Wallace murder, *The Man From The Pru* (1990) starring Jonathan Pryce and Susanna York. It's not known whether the additional scenes were required because of the substantial location filming in each episode, but the format of the serial differs from the usual course of a conspiracy thriller. Usually the hero is confronted with a mystery and we only gradually get to a glimpse of the people behind the plot. But *Spyship* introduces the people behind the plot in the first half hour. In a way it plays fair with the viewer because we see the conspiracy develop in real time although some crucial elements are withheld. In addition the interplay between Main, Simon, Hilmore and the last-minute introduction of Strang is so obscure that it can distract from the central mystery.

Even when first broadcast there was a slight sense of deja vu in Richard Harvey's folky title song (performed by June Tabor) which comes across as a knock-off of Clannad's theme from *Harry's Game* (1982). The serial seems to be treading similarly flattened ground in the scenes with Peter Eyre and David Burke strolling around the more arcane tourist sites of London discussing British history. Even the casting of Don Henderson and Thorley Walters from *Strangers* and Michael Aldridge playing yet another security service chief (viz *Tinker, Tailor..*, and the *Power Game* episode *The Goose Chase*).

The scenes outside of London have a stronger narrative because of the search for the truth. We the viewers have seen something sinister happen to the *Caistor* although we don't know exactly what has happened. The city is never actually named as Hull, although the city and University scenes were filmed in Hull. The portside scenes were filmed in Grimsby as Hull's St Andrews Dock (where the *Gaul* sailed from) had already been closed and redeveloped into a retail centre). With a limited budget, the production sketches the uncertainty, dread and disbelief of the trawler's loss. The wives and mothers of the trawlermen are well represented with a lack of sentimentality. There's a whole micro-drama in the first couple of episodes around the character played by Malcolm Hebden (Norris from *Coronation Street*) trying to mount a search for the wreckage and his harridan of a mother played by Jean Boht (*Bread*), who asks why it couldn't have been him, rather than his brother who died.

There's also a good deal of gallows humour. During the Inquiry, one of the wives shouts Martin over, *"Come and sit here with the rich widows!"* Unsurprisingly, no-one tries to do a Hull accent (when he played a trawler skipper in <u>The Seventh Wave</u> even Patrick Wymark was criticised for getting the Grimsby accent wrong), and the odd bits of dialect seem closer to Tyneside. It's notable that the engineer who has to be taken off with a broken leg was the first TV role of Jimmy Naill.

While the London scenes can be annoying (because they seem to distract from the ongoing search for the truth) they do have some humour. When discussing the marine scientist Dowdall, Main is annoyed that their usual "sympathetic" scientist is not preparing the report on the life buoy. The young and eager Simon says that Dowdall has an *"Awful lot of letters after his name."*. Main agrees, *"FAR too many for this line of work."*. There's also an amusing pantomime when Main strides into his outer office leaving the door wide open. His secretary immediately gets up and firmly shuts the door. Main continues into his inner office, where he opens the safe door and removes some files. He begins to discuss the plot with Simon leaving the safe door open. During the course of the conversation, a porter walks into Main's office, sees the open safe door, pointedly shuts and locks it and walks out again, barely acknowledged by Main and Simon (later on, when Main is caught out by Hilmore, the same porter will steer Main to Hilmore's office like a school prefect). Yet despite the odd amusing highlight, there is a generic familiarity about the London scenes (ITV would begin showing *Chessgame* halfway through *Spyship's* run starring Terence Stamp as Anthony Price's counterintelligence agent Dr David Audley) .

The role of journalist Martin Taylor was only Tom Wilkinson's third TV role and his first lead (although he had been acting since 1974 with the Nottingham Playhouse and National Theatre). Martin seems an unlikely hero, deeply withdrawn. In the opening scenes, as they leave the Minerva pub Jonno says the people in the pub are his friends, but he doesn't know if Martin is his friend (a subtle point is that the only time Martin calls out to his father, he calls him *Jonno*, rather than *Dad*) Jonno tells his son that he knows he's unhappy,*"Moping about, always on your own."* but, *"I don't know you - because you never tell me ow't."* We learn that Martin did not visit often before his mother's funeral. When they return to Jonno's house, Martin is surprised to find a postcard on the mantlepiece that he sent home from Greece when he was at University. Johnno says off-handedly that he doesn't know how long it's been up there, and says he'd like to sail somewhere warm, just once.

Later, the recently divorced Suzy (who works in the University labs), says of Martin that it makes a change to have a date with someone who *"likes talking"*, suggesting that it's just his dad - or people like his parents- who Martin can't talk to . In the final episode, in a state of exhaustion, he confesses to the Norwegian journalist who is sheltering him that, *"I loved my parents - but I never really knew them as an adult."*. Born in the 1950's Martin appears to have the typical estrangement of working class boys who went to Grammar School on a scholarship and who were taught to behave differently from their background but at the same time knew that they didn't really belong in the upper class. The bigger question is where he develops the resilience to survive the conspiracy against him. After he's fended off one attack by Evans, Suzy says, *"What really bothers me is it doesn't seem to affect you. Nothing does really."* Martin's too young to have done National Service, but we can perhaps assume that during his working class childhood (especially marked as *different*), he learnt to instinctively defend himself. This enables him to survive three murder attempts by Evans and finally kill the assassin during a fight that happens so quickly it could almost be an accident.

Martin's partner in the investigation is Suzy, who Lesley Nightingale makes adorable. Lesley had appeared briefly in *Muck and Brass* as Mel Smith's secretary and appeared in *Boys From The Black Stuff* as the social worker who gets head butted by Yosser Hughes' young daughter. We learn most about Suzy from other people. Johnno tells Martin that Suzy was like a daughter to him and his wife (perhaps a hint of reproach to Martin who was not like a son). A work colleague says Suzy has *"had a lot of practice.."* getting over men, even though *"she's so mature in other ways.* If Martin is the typically alienated working class Grammar School boy, Suzy is representative of those working class Grammar School and University graduates who found their options as financially constrained (albeit in a less manual job) as if they'd left school at 15. We learn that Suzy feels trapped in the University lab- *"Even with a damn good degree, there's nowhere else I can go to get a job."* As it becomes clear that the truth is being hidden, Suzy helps Martin by using the resources of the University to track down Dowdall's unedited report and get in touch with the wife of Captain Huniger. Ultimately, Suzy almost pays the ultimate price when Evans attacks and terrorises her to find out where Martin is hiding. Although hospitalised, Suzy survives, though perhaps because Evans is saving her for later. There's an eerie scene in episode three where the assassin is prowling round her empty flat and rubs her silk dressing gown against his cheek before sniffing it. And when he prepare to terrorise her in episode five we see Evans stroking a Punk-style poster of a woman biting a whip.

The third lead character is Francis Main, although he only emerges obliquely during the first episode. Peter Eyre was already a well-established stage actor, having appeared in Spike Milligan's *Son of Oblomov* in 1964 and played major roles for the Nottingham Playhouse, Royal Shakespeare Company and Birmingham Repertory. He had generally played supporting roles on film and TV such Tesman in *Hedda* (1975) opposite *Glenda Jackson* , and a university lecturer working for the KGB in a 1972 episode of *Callan*. Eyre's inscrutable performance as Main matches the enigmatic script and it's therefore only in retrospect that we appreciate the character's journey. At times, Francis Main's situation is the same as a character in a series like *The Power Game*. When Hilmore tells Main to provide wreckage from the *Caistor*, when Main has already told the Russians there won't be any wreckage, he's in the same position as any other middle-manager made to look foolish because of a senior management about turn. Similarly, when Evans starts to go out of control, we don't immediately appreciate the risk this puts Main in. It's not surprising in his 1990 adaptation of *House of Cards*, Andrew Davies adopted the device of Francis Urquhart talking to the audience, taking them into his confidence and explaining his devious schemes. .

Evans was played by Philip Hynd, who acted in series such as *Bergerac* and *Fell Tiger*, before shifting to a successful career as a Change Management Consultant where he helped Pfizer bring Viagra to market nine months ahead of schedule. Evans is one of a team of ex-soldiers who Main controls to carry out dirty-tricks operations. He appears abstemious and self-possessed, often seen jogging through the countryside (even in Norway). As Hilmore notes, Evans is probably smarter than the others. His contact address is only an anonymous drop for his cash payments. When Evans learns how much Martin knows, he tells Main that he's been taping their telephone conversations as insurance (*"I'm not on a pension. I don't want my name to be given to some bloke in a telephone box."*) and forces Main to sanction Martin's murder. Described by Hilmore as, *"Embarrassing enough to warrant execution,"* and throws away his radio-receiver when Hilmore tries to shut him down. Hynd delivers some of the most unsettling scenes in the serial - especially his Peter Manuel-like prowling around Suzy's empty flat, helping himself to a cup of water as he scans the kitchen for props to terrorise her. In the end, Martin shares the audience's frustration that Evans' downfall is quick and offscreen - almost accidental.

Considering the script, the biggest elephant in the room is probably why Hull-based writer Alan Plater was not approached to do the adaptation. Jarrow-born, but living in Hull from an early age, Plater had written a 1973 *Play For Today* set in Hull (*The Land of Green Ginger)* had written for crime series such as *Z Cars* and also worked on the thriller *Juggernaut* (1974). Although he had been doing a lot of work with Yorkshire TV, he was obviously available to the BBC at the time as he adapted John McNeil's computer crime thriller *The Consultant* , which was broadcast on BBC1 in June 1983. Plater had also written his 'anti-thriller' *Get Lost* for ITV in 1981, which would morph into 1985's *The Beiderbecke Affair* featuring down-to-earth schoolteacher heroes similar in some ways to Martin and Suzy. It would have been interesting to see what Plater made of *Spyship* although as it is, Plater later adapted Chris Mullin's conspiracy thriller, *A Very British Coup*(1988).

The TV serial *does*, in the end, provide a solution to the mystery. Almost veering into science fiction, the solution is a case of *"what can go wrong, did go wrong"* - with both sides equally guilty, and the crew of the trawler innocent bystanders. Hilmore tells Martin that NATO and the Soviets are like two men in a darkened room, separated by a wall. They fear each other, but they learn that by turning on a light and peering over the wall,they can see what the other is doing. When Martin questions the lives of the trawler crew, Hilmore replies that there are *"Hundreds, thousands, dying the most hideous deaths every day. All they have is fear. Indignation is a luxury."*. Given time to consider whether he will keep the story secret, Martin tells Suzy that even if he published, *People expect it. They know there's a war going on constantly, which they never see. If it doesn't affect the daily routine of their lives, what the hell, it's forgotten."*

SPYSHIP AND THE STORY OF THE GAUL

"For Norman the starting point was always - what are 'they' not asking?" Obituary of Norman Felton (1)

In February 1974, the stern trawler *Gaul* disappeared in the Barents Sea, North of Norway. The verdict of the official inquiry was that it was swamped in heavy seas.

From the start, there was intense press interest in the story. Although a BBC investigation was abandoned, Thames TV's *This Week* ran a two part film. Thursday 16 October 1975 saw the first part of *The Mystery of The Gaul*, researched by Tom Keene and Brian Haynes and produced by Norman Fenton. This ended with the statement that evidence suggested that the life buoy purporting to come from the *Gaul* had been planted at sea. The second episode, on Thursday 23rd October, picked up on the 'spyship' rumours, disagreed with the official verdict that that the vessel had been swamped and concluded it had either been accidentally or deliberately struck by a submarine.

In 1994, following the collapse of the Soviet Union, Norman Fenton produced another documentary for the Channel Four *Dispatches* series restating this theory. In August 1997, Norman Fenton chartered a survey vessel (financed by Anglia Television and Norwegian broadcaster NRK) which quickly located the wreckage, still in one piece. On 6 November 1997, the results of this survey were broadcast on the Channel 4 *Dispatches* , "Secrets of the Gaul." As a result, Hull MP and Deputy Prime Minister John Prescott ordered a new enquiry (including a new survey of the wreck in 1998). In 2004, a Report into the Re-opened Formal Investigation into the Loss of the FV Gaul was published by the Wreck Commissioner, Mr Justice David Steel.

The report notes that no search was made for the wreck before 1997, because the authorities believed they knew why the ship had sunk and that any wreck would be very difficult to find. Therefore it would have been a waste of public funds to search for the wreck. *"Mr Felton's success in discovering the wreck quickly and at no great expense completely undermined (the official stance) and refuelled suspicion."* The report acknowledges that the original decision not to search for the wreck *"caused the gravest dismay to the relatives (and) encouraged the belief in the theory that the vessel had been captured by the Russians.* The report acknowledges that suspicions were raised because the *Gaul* was only two years old, two sister vessels survived the same storm, there was no SOS call and no floating wreckage.

Using the official report, it is possible to compare the storyline of *Spyship* with what is now believed to have happened to the *Gaul*.

TV The *Caistor* is a lone vessel chartered by Harding (Malcolm Tierney). **Fact** The *Gaul* was one of four sister vessels in the British United Trawlers fleet, two of which were also in the Barents Sea. It had been built for the Ranger Fishing Company of North Shields as the *Ranger Castor* (the novel called the vessel *Mary Castor*, whereas the TV trawler is named after the Lincolnshire village of Caistor) and renamed *Gaul* when Ranger Fishing was taken over by British United Trawlers. The fact that two of the sister vessels survived the same storm added to the suspicions about the sinking of the *Gaul*.

TV The *Caistor* is a stern trawler (the fishing net is dropped from the rear, rather than the side). **Fact** The *Gaul* was a stern factory trawler ship, with an additional factory deck and crew to process and freeze the catch.

TV Metcalfe (Jimmy Naill) breaks his leg during the voyage and has to be taken off the *Caistor* at a port in Norway. The wireless operator asks him to take a letter to his wife. **Fact** The regular mate of the *Gaul* was taken ill and left the vessel at Lodigen (a replacement was taken on at Tromso).

TV The *Caistor* is diverted from its normal fishing ground to spy on the Soviets with the Intercept Receivers. **Fact** The *Gaul* had been fishing alongside its sister vessel *Kelt*. The *Kelt* lost sight of the *Gaul* at 20:30 on the 7th February but the *Gaul* reported being laid up to repair a damaged net. By 02:00 on 8th February, the *Kelt* and another vessel had to lay and dodge (*at a standstill, without power*) due to bad weather. The *Gaul* also reported 'laid and dodging'.This was the last report heard from the *Gaul*.

After the end of the 'Cold War', the 2004 report established that on three occasions in the 1960's a trawler had been chartered to make trips with specialist staff and equipment. The skipper was indemnified against any loss of catch while following the course requested by the Navy. On two occasions, trawlers were used to search for a missing Soviet test missile, although the ships officers were told that they were looking for a camera from a US sub. The mate of one of these vessels, was later the mate of the Gaul. Not surprisingly, there was common gossip about spying missions.

TV *Caistor* disappears during a storm without sending an SOS. **Fact** The *Gaul* was last sighted by another fishing vessel on the 8th February during a Force 10 storm and disappeared between 8th and 9th February 1974 without sending a distress signal

TV There is an eight day search by the Royal Navy and Norwegian military. **Fact** An operation was mounted by the Royal Navy, RAF and Norwegian authorities between 11th and 15th February. A subsequent air search between 21 and 22 February failed to find any trace.

TV Tom Silvers (Malcolm Hebden), the brother of one of the crew, starts fundraising to charter a search for wreckage from the *Caistor*. Francis Main and Evans frame him for theft. **Fact** In March 1974, a freelance journalist proposed a search for the wreck of the *Gaul*.He was not accused of theft. The vessel owners refused to contribute to the costs of the search and the official view was that any wreck would be difficult to find.

TV The Russians plant a life buoy from the **Caistor** off the coast of Norway. It is found by a two-man fishing vessel with a dodgy captain who only sails at the weekend. **Fact** A life buoy from the *Gaul* was found off the Norwegian coast on 8 May 1974 by a Norwegian whaling vessel.

TV As noted above, the *Caistor* had no sister vessels. **Fact** Inspection of two of the sister vessels of the *Gaul* found rust in the water-tight doors and hatches. In the *Kurd*, rust and overpainting meant that the door to the watertight door to the factory could not be closed. This could have indicated a concern in the *Gaul* but the official Department of Trade view in 1974 appears to have been that, since the *Gaul* had not been inspected, this could only be a supposition. In the wider community, the fact that two of the sister vessels survived the storm in the Barents Sea generated further suspicion about the loss of the Gaul.

TV It's not stated when the Formal Investigation at City Hall begins, although it appears to be very soon after the loss of the *Caistor*. **Fact** The Official Formal Investigation lasting 14 days, began on 17 September at Hull City Hall.

TV Relatives of the crew disrupt the OFI saying the Russians have got the crew for spying. **Fact** This happened on the first day of the OFI.

TV Fielding (Don Henderson), from the Trawler Owners Guild tells Tom that, *"They've got to dream up summat, they've got to hope that their fellers are still alive...trawlermen are at sea for months at a time. They get bored. Talk. It's just fancy."* **Fact** The report notes that, *"rumours almost immediately began to spread that the disappearance of the vessel and her crew could only be attributable to the fact (or the belief) that the **Gaul** was involved in espionage and had fallen into Russian hands."*(page 73)

TV A local Labour MP asks a question in the House about Russian involvement. Hilmore tells Main that, *"The Prime Minister had to make an unprepared statement."*. **Fact**. James Johnson, one of the three Hull MP's, met with the Under Secretary of State for Trade, where the question of Russian involvement was raised and denied. In July 1974, another Hull MP John Prescott asked whether British Navy personnel had ever sailed on trawlers. Bill Rogers MP, the Parliamentary Under Secretary for the Navy, confirmed that Navy personnel did travel on trawlers *"to gain seagoing experience,"* but made it clear that there were none travelling on the *Gaul*. (The affirmative reply was leaked to the press creating a *"Spy Ship Storm*) Rogers later added that, apart from officers attached to the Royal Navy Fishery Protection Service getting practical experience in how trawlers worked, there had been two occasions when officers from the Hydrographical Service took part in exercises to check the radio navigation chain by reference to the satellite navigation service *"and to try and find some equipment that had been lost."* As the report notes, it was known in the Hull fishing industry that the response was *economical with the truth*" when it said that, *"the British trawler fleet is not involved in any way with intelligence* *gathering."* (In a 1997 TV documentary, Lord Rogers explained that he had been misled by his officials).

TV - Admiralty scientist Dowdall (Thorley Walters) deduces that the buoy has never been in deep water. He refuses to tone down his report, but Main's assistant Simon (Paul Geoffrey) prepares a rewritten version for the inquiry. **Fact** The analyst from the Admiralty Materials Lab remarked upon the absences of deep water diatoms and presence of fresh water diatoms. The 2004 report noted that the analyst gave evidence on Day 5 of the OFI and had admitted that lack of solar illumination could have led to the absence of deep water plankton, although the presence of fresh water fauna could not be explained and this discrepancy was made much of by the Thames TV *This Week* documentaries.

TV *The issue of the life buoy directly contradicts what happened in fact and suspicion about the buoy was one of the main themes of the* **This Week** *TV documentaries.* **Fact** *However, the 2004 report notes that the Surveyor who identified the rusted doors and hatches on the sister vessels of the* **Gaul** *felt aggrieved that his evidence had been downplayed by the Department of Trade. His findings on the sister vessels were not covered in his examination at the inquiry. The inquiry did not consider the possibility that the condition of the ship might have contributed to its sinking, even though it would have supported the official explanation that the ship was overwhelmed. Only when the wreck was finally located did examination support the Surveyor's theory that the ship was not watertight. So, far from allaying the Spyship rumours, the suppression of this theory helped to create the Spyship myth. Could the Spyship rumour actually have been politically convenient?*

The 2004 report gives the probable cause of the loss of the Gaul as the factory deck flooding with the capsize as a result of a sudden and sharp turn to port under full power. *The report notes that there were no statutory requirements for structural strength, watertight integrity or stability. Although an enabling act had been passed following the loss of three vessels in 1968*, it was not until 1975, after the Gaul disappeared, that the Fishing Vessels (Safety Provision) Rules 1975 came into effect. In short, there was no political will to ensure that trawlers were as safe as they could have been.*

As noted above, the security characters in Spyship are often in the same position as management characters in The Plane Makers and The Power Game. Main is made to look a fool by Hilmore's decision about planting the life buoy, Hilmore tells Main to make sure there is no evidence left, but doesn't want anything to be traceable back to him. When Hilmore tells Simon to make sure the analyst Dowdall is kept quiet, Simon makes positive noises but doesn't tell Main that he'd already bungled a previous attempt to keep the scientist on-side. In this way, the serial addresses the main objection to any conspiracy thriller; Why would anyone go to such lethal and explosive lengths to cover something up, knowing the truth will probably always emerge? The serial follows the cock-up theory.When we eventually learn what has happened to the Caistor, the cause of the disaster is a combination of unplanned reactions to unforseen events. Literally what can go wrong, will go wrong.. Similarly, the conspiracy mounts because of individuals pursuing their self-interest and making hasty reactions to unforseen events. There is no all-seeing conspiracy, only farce.

(1) Obituary of Norman Fenton August 14 2013
https://swimminginstormyweather.wordpress.com/tag/norman-fenton/

The Headscarf Revolutionaries and The Luckiest 13 – Triple Trawler Tales by Brian W. Lavery.

The Headscarf Revolutionaries, **Brian W Lavery's fascinating account of the loss of three trawlers in 1968 and the campaign by trawlermen's wives to change the shipping laws tells two compelling stories.** The first is the against the odds survival of Harry Eddom after his trawler went down in a winter storm off the coast of Iceland. The second is the decision of a few Hull women to stick their necks out and defy the community for the greater good.

Today it's fashionable to be scathing about Health and Safety culture, but the revolution that Lillian Bilocca and her "army" campaigned for included ensuring that every ship had a radio operator. In 1968 it was still possible for a trawler to sail without a qualified radio operator. When that happened, the skipper would have to double-up as radio man, sometimes with a transmitter that had to be coaxed into life on ships with poor design. At Christmas, when experienced trawlermen wanted to be with their families, ships often sailed with unskilled crews attracted by quick money. Ice was a constant hazard, threatening to weigh down the vessel or put the radar scanner out of action. The ice could only be cleared by a crewman hacking away at it while someone held his ankles to make sure he wasn't swept overboard.

In January and February 1968, three Hull trawlers went down in as many weeks, claiming the lives of 58 men. Lillian Bilocca, employed as a fish skinner ("filleting was men's work") decided to raise a petition to improve safety on the trawlers. "We need to take action, " she said, "I have a bag packed.I'll go anywhere, anytime.I'll board any unsafe trawler in the country to stop an unsafe ship sailing." The publicity resulting from the demands of "the headscarf revolutionaries" stirred the highest levels of Government into putting safety measures into effect. But there is no feelgood factor about the story. Lillian Bilocca was not the sole mind behind the revolution (trawlerman's daughter Yvonne Blenkinsop quickly articulated the safety measures that were lacking and skippers wife Mary Denness ensured that the Hessle Road Womens' Committee was not just a management v labour movement), but she paid the highest price. She was sacked from her fish processing job, and became effectively unemployable. After an appearance on ABC TV's Eamonn Andrews Show (11th February 1968) she received hate mail to rival the venom of internet trolls, "One..signed with an indecipherable scrawl..the ugly flourish of the scrawl gave the impression that its writer could not get the hate on the page quickly enough."

And while safety was improved on the trawlers, no-one could guess that within five years, the fishing industry would be devastated by Iceland's imposition of a 200 mile fishing ban. Nevertheless, we can only speculate how many more lives might have been lost in those five years without the action of the Hessle Road women. The precariousness of the fishing industry underlines the difficulty the women had in demanding change. Skippers were rewarded by how much fish they could catch. Even with a radio operator on board they might maintain radio silence to stop rivals cutting in on a good fishing ground. Fishing was seen as the concern of men. Yvonne

Blenkinsop was punched in the face in a restaurant and told to "keep yer fuckin nose out of men's business". But a lot of the opposition also came from women, who thought that the "Headscarf Revolutionaries" were a threat to the industry. Yet set against all these issues is the remarkable story of Harry Eddom. Knocked unconscious by an inflating lifeboat as the sea turned the Ross Cleveland over, he was hauled aboard by two crewmates. After nine hours in mountainous icy seas, the raft was hurled onto a rocky Icelandic beach. By now the only survivor, Eddom began walking through a blizzard to try and find shelter. An incredible story of fate and resilience. This is an incredibly rewarding book, not only for the stories it tells but also for the picture it creates of our recent history - a time when union leaders had grown up fighting in the Spanish Civil War, when men could still be jailed for refusing to sail and reporters could introduce themselves as being, "from the World's Greatest Newspaper.."   The Headscarf Revolutionaries Lillian Bilocca and the Hull Triple-Trawler Disaster Brian W Lavery _Barbican Press 2015 ISBN 978-1-909954-14-4

The Luckiest Thirteen - **"The word 'prequel' grates with me," says Brian W Lavery, but he acknowledges that this is very much the *Zulu Dawn* to *The Headscarf Revolutionaries,* his trailblazing account of the 1968 campaign by Hull trawlermen's wives to change the shipping laws in the wake of three trawler sinkings.**

Although published in 2015, *Revolutionaries* seemed to be the hot fuse of Hull's *City of Culture* year with its Ibsen-esque heroines inspiring street paintings, stage plays and TV documentaries. *The Luckiest Thirteen* takes us back even earlier to Christmas 1966 and the story of *St Finbarr*, a state-of-the-art trawler which erupted into flames in the middle of a fierce storm in Newfoundland waters. The crew numbered twenty-five and the survivors would be the 'luckiest thirteen.'

The St Finbarr was a new type of distant water trawler, designed to go further, sail longer, and hold more fish than its rivals. Instead of being back-breakingly gutted on deck, and smothered in ice in an attempt to keep them fresh, fish were deboned and frozen in blocks below decks in a factory process designed to optimise the amount of saleable fish delivered back to port. Powered by fuel-efficient Hawker Siddeley engines and equipped with the latest Rediffusion electronics, the St Finbarr was an ocean-going realisation of Harold Wilson's *"White Heat of Technology.* But on Christmas Day 1966, the ship was battling against icy swirling gales and a 'confused sea'. The captain had been at the helm more than eighteen hours, holding the ship steady against the shifting waves. Suddenly, smoke and flames burst out of nowhere, driving the exhausted crew back up to the freezing upper deck.

The Luckiest Thirteen tells the story of the crew, the fire and the aftermath. It reminds us of how prose can still be superior to film in capturing brief, confusing, life-or-death situations such as the disorientated stumbling of men roused from sleep by choking smoke. Lavery uses a clear, but constantly-shifting point of view to capture the cruel unpredictable risk of the frost-bitten climb up a rope-ladder to a rescuing ship.

This meticulously researched history moves along with the pace of a novel, recreating a world where the tragedy would go unreported for hours because newspapers and even TV news shut down for the festive period. The book follows the Superintendant of the Mission for Deep Sea Fishermen, and the reporters of the *Hull Daily Mail* as they begin their separate visits to the relatives.

Brian Lavery depicts a bygone world of "three day millionaires" and the vivid characters who captained the trawlers. Of the St Finbarr captain, Tom Sawyers he writes that, *"In often-atrocious weather Sawyers pushed the ship and crew into areas of the Labrador coast, which caused the men to question and even curse him. But time after time the nets came back bursting-full. The crew did not know how to take Sawyers...in one breath, he could be kind, almost avuncular to young deckhands...but in a heartbeat, could flash into Bligh-like rage."*. Lavery also recounts the legend of Philip Gay, skipper of the Ross Cleveland, who was confronted by a drunken mutiny when he tried to close the on-board bonded liquor store. After a crewman grabbed the key to "the Bond", Gay left the mess, only to return a few minutes later to lay out the man who had grabbed the key. As the crew moved towards Gay, *"they noticed the weapon in his hand. He raised it and pointed it at the crew. It was the gun used to launch flares - and it was loaded."*

The fishing skippers were determined men. And after the crew had been ordered to abandon ship, Tom Sawyers, his First Mate Walt Collier and Chief Engineer Hughie Williams elected to stay on board. While the ship was insured, the catch was not, and they gambled that they could keep the ship afloat long enough for it to be towed back into port before the cargo defrosted.

Lavery delivers a satisfying third act with coverage of the Board of Trade inquiry, almost a year after the sinking of the St Finbarr, which tried to establish the cause of the disaster. In the adversarial system, owners, contractors and survivors try to defend their actions while maritime lawyer Dr Lionel Rosen, representing the bereaved families attempts to *"harry and bully (them) into accepting some culpability for the loss of some of the twelve lives."*. The powerful afterword reminds us that no-one really walks away from a disaster without scars.

The Luckiest Thirteen The Forgotten Men of St Finbarr Brian W Lavery _Barbican Press 2017   ISBN 9781909954229

Eggs or Anarchy: The Brexit No Deal Breakfast

17 August 2019

Now that we are assured that Britain will exit the EU in October, deal-or-no-deal, I have been reading what will surely become essential reading. Eggs or Anarchy by William Sitwell is the story of Lord Woolton, World War Two Minister of Food, who ensured that Britain kept eating as supply chains seized up and resources dwindled.

Frederick James Marquis was joint managing director of the Lewis department store chain. It was a little known fact that Marquis had grown up in a poor terraced street in Salford. As Sitwell notes, modern politicians would, "barely let an interview pass without eulogising on their near poverty-stricken roots (but) Woolton never mentioned his very real, unassuming origins, indeed he rather buried them."

Educated at Manchester Grammar School and Manchester College of Technology, Marquis' career took a path through social work, teaching and journalism before being invited by Sir Rex Cohen to join the Lewis firm. One of Marquis' personal goals was to achieve success in business while respecting his social conscience.

Such was the reputation Fred Marquis achieved in business that, on the outbreak of war, he was appointed Minister of Food. Marquis had already achieved success in cutting through red tape as a technical advisor to the War Office, ensuring that sufficient uniforms were produced to clothe the influx of servicemen.

Ennobled as Lord Woolton, his task was a stiff one. Britain had been a net importer of food: "half of all meat, three-quarters of all cheese, cereals, fats and sugars and four-fifths of fruit came from overseas." With enemy submarines sinking shipping and former exporters over-run, those supply chains were at threat. On 29 September 1939, the Ministry of Food began a registration scheme to record the details of every civilian in the land – men, women and children. This provided the basis of a rationing scheme, which would ensure that food was evenly distributed. At the same time Woolton set his civil servants to studying the nutritional requirements set by the League of Nations to determine how calories the country needed to keep going. Behind the cold science, Fred Marquis never forgot his experience growing up in Salford – his knowledge of just what the working classes really ate.

Woolton had many critics – members of the House of Lords were particularly fond in quoting anecdotal tales of how his food distribution lines were failing while the press eagerly reported how Black Marketers were getting around the rules. Woolton also had to contend with the strong farmers lobby which was dissatisfied with the prices set for their produce.

But Woolton prevailed with a gift for plain-speaking and determination. "Here was a man not pleading for their support so he could keep his job. And here was a man who talked to them with an honesty they did not expect from politicians."

Woolton was also a tough but canny negotiator with suppliers. Argentina tried to push an above-market price for its beef, perceiving Britain to have no alternatives. "The British could moralise and talk about principles all they liked, but they had no choice but to pay up." Woolton informed the Ambassador that he accepted their decision, but since they could no longer trade, he would order British supply ships to stop calling at Argentinian ports. Since Argentina's cold stores were stacked with produce, and British ships were part of the country's import-export supply chain, this would cost Argentina millions. The Ambassador conceded, but then Woolton told him to raise his price by a small margin. "Woolton wanted final recognition of the negotiation to belong to the Ambassador, so that he could claim to his government that Britain was a reasonable country to deal with: a satisfied supplier meant that they would continue to sell to him as a customer."

Sitwell concludes that, "Britain, at the end of the war, was not just in good physical shape, it had – and has never been – so healthy....child mortality had never been so low and far fewer mothers died in childbirth. Fewer babies had been stillborn and children were both taller and studier. There was also a markedly lower rate of tooth decay. All...achieved with fewer doctors, dentists, nurses and health visitors. While the rich ate less, the poorer ate more adequately."

While the British have never forgotten the ordeal of food-rationing and how 'we' all came through it together, the man who won the commitment of civil servants and tradesmen and ensured that the nation came through it healthier than before is unjustly forgotten. Even the 'Lord Woolton Pie', created by a Savoy Chef to popularise the use of root vegetables and wholemeal flour is little celebrated. But with the prospect of crashing out on World Trade Organisation rules looms, perhaps a copy of Eggs or Anarchy should be delivered to every member of Boris Johnson's 'war cabinet'.

Eggs or Anarchy by William Sitwell Simon and Shuster 2016 ISBN 978-1-4711-510

My Brilliant Career as A Ghost Hunter

The great thing about the late 1980's was that everything was marketable – even the afterlife.

When I was a kid, I dreamed of being a magician like Doctor Strange, using spells from ancient tomes to prise open the locks of nature. But the 1980's revealed that the true magicians were the accountants – their ancient grimoires were ledger books, the mystic incantations were Ponzi schemes. Instead of fracturing reality with a Steve Ditko special effect, the true sleight of hand was a leveraged buyout. In days gone by it took a fraudulent medium with cheesecloth and floating tambourines to relieve the credulous of their cash. By the 1980's, all that was needed was an investment promoter with a video presentation and slick prospectus.

But it took my pal, Mickey Cavicci to bring the two together with Para-Psych Investigations. His electroplated tongue convinced investors that there was a hungry market out there waiting to be serviced. On the hamburger level of the supernatural was the equivalent of Pay Day loan customers, willing to enter into a financial commitment to satisfy a deep-rooted need. Moving up to the smaller, but more financially rewarding core of Berni Inn customers, were those who in later years would divert their disposable income to nailbars, Botox injections or cosmetic dental work. And then there was ultimate goal of some company or educational establishment willing to squander its resources on a search for the afterlife.

Considerable thought was put into our office. We ensure our doorway was not too intimidating for the Hamburger clientele, but not too 'common' for the Berni Inn crowd. Ceiling to floor curtains over the window – thin enough to let the light in, but opaque enough to create an aura of mystery and confidentiality. Subdued purple mood lighting in the corners, pre-fitted strip lights overhead. Contemporary desk and chairs on hire, and a state-of-the-art Amstrad word processor providing a reassuring note of modernity to offset the gothic photographs on the wall.

The business strategy was to aim for a 40% clear-up rate for the sake of credibility. Reassure both the clearly deluded Hamburger customer and the neurotic Berni Inn client as quickly as possible, getting them out of door on a cloud of conviviality so that they could go out and spread the word about our unbiased service as quickly as possible. It was a bit like seduction ; only the customers who knew what they were letting themselves in for would be strung out into a long-term relationship.

As far as "haunted houses" went, I soon found that it paid to sub-contract to an experience builder. Every building has a life-cycle. Or as J.E. Gordon put it, "All structures will be broken or destroyed in the end – just as all people will die in the end. It is the purpose of medicine and engineering to postpone these occurrences for a decent interval."* Far too often the inhabitants give the building the equivalent of plastic surgery but neglect the structure. The ancient reproach and laments sensed by the dwellers of haunted houses were often the result of the decaying soul of the building. A quick survey by an experienced builder would often identify the source of the discontent.

J.E.Gordon, Structures (Penguin 1978) page 324

I've laid this all out in pretty cold-blooded terms. You're probably coming up with objections and there's probably nothing I didn't say to myself over the three years until the bubble burst. There were, and probably still are, a lot of people who want to believe there is something on the other side of the door. How far was I helping them? How far was I exploiting them? I some ways, I was no different from a bookie, responding to a need. But then the limit of a bookie's interaction was taking money off people over a counter – I was having to interact with them on a deeper level, trying to read what they really wanted out of our service before deciding whether to consign them to the 40% clear up quota or string them out for longer. And, I forgot to mention that Mickey employed a team of telesales girls from his other activities to field any phone enquiries and promise them the universe.

The case that really sticks in my mind is one of the first. It ended up being part of the 40% clear-up cases, but that was nothing to do with me.

Mickey was excited because It looked like it might be the big one. A chemical plant up north was having trouble in one of its new labs. People were feeling disturbed and had even started seeing things. It had been low key so far, but the management wanted to clamp down while it was still summer. They didn't want hysteria to spread into the dark winter afternoons.

I drove over with Bronco, our tame builder, the next Saturday. It was a dull overcast day, and although there were only maintenance shifts in the plant, there was still a constant howl of processes in the background. The important thing is that no-one was working in the pre-fabricated buildings that held the haunted lab, so we could do our checks in secret. We were met by the production manager who was clearly under orders to get this problem sorted, whatever he might have thought about our competence. "One thing you can be sure of. It's nothing to do with chemicals from the plant. The lab windows are sealed and we've done belt-and-braces checks for that kind of thing." Even so ,this was the 1980's, so the health and safety induction went as far as the instruction to run in the same direction as everyone else if an alarm went off.

As Bronco ran his checks over the main structure of the lab, I applied my limited knowledge to the office section where most of the sightings had been reported. It was stuffy because the windows had to be sealed shut, and even with the primitive air conditioning going full blast, I became aware of a sense of oppression. As if I wasn't alone.

Towards twelve, Bronco moved into the office area and after a couple of minutes I could tell he'd found something. With a look of sly satisfaction, he looked at his watch and said he was going to drive into town and fetch some fish and chips. I knew it was pointless trying to ask him what he'd found. He preferred to let me spend a good half-hour trying to guess the answer so that his expertise would be unchallenged when he whipped the silk scarf away to reveal the rabbit. I reminded Bronco that the production manager had said we could eat free at the staff canteen, but Bronco pointed out that if we did that we wouldn't be able to claim the expenses back.

Even so, I was feeling both chilled and sweaty and still had the sense of being observed. I certainly didn't fancy staying in the lab on my own, so as Bronco drove off, I stopped outside the prefabricated buildings to get a bit of what passed for fresh air. As I traced the yellow lines marking the "safe pavement", I turned the corner and spotted something incongruous. Behind the metal pipelines and beneath a cooling tower, there was a small Victorian manor house. I couldn't help stepping over the yellow lines, onto the pitted tarmac to get a closer look. It was an old house with no sign of life. The only sound was the drone of the factory. I got the feeling I was being watched, but couldn't see any faces in the uncurtained windows.

Suddenly, I glanced behind me. There was a worker in overalls and hard hat, his eyes fixed on me. I was embarrassed to realise I'd been caught breaking the rules, walking in the process area, but he didn't seem too bothered. I tried to excuse my breach by babbling on about how remarkable the sight of the building was.

He laughed and explained the "big house" was used as offices. It had once been the home of the local Earl. The story went that the post war Labour government had done a compulsory purchase on the surrounding land to build the much-needed chemical plant. Although others said the Earl's family were absentee landlords down in London by then, and had squeezed a good price out of the company for the house. But if the government had expected the chemical firm to eradicate this last trace of the aristocracy, they had mis-judged the executives who thought the "big house" would make a fine setting for their offices. It had been that way for 30 or 40 years but now the management consultants eviscerating the company had decided it was better to flatten the house and use the space to expand production facilities. So now it just stood empty, condemned, awaiting the bulldozers.

When Bronco returned, he explained his theory over pie and chips. He put his spirit level against the wall of the office space. The bubble trembled slightly. There was some kind of vibration coming from the air conditioning. It was an effect that had first been noticed in the 1970's – infrasound (or low frequency noise as I believe we have to call it today) – too low to hear, but generating feelings of unease and hallucinations.

It was likely the fan in the air conditioning unit had been thrown off its centre of gravity. A build up of dust could do it. Of course, it was just a theory. The scientific approach would be to test it with specialised equipment. And we knew Micky would want to spin this out into an exhaustive and expensive investigation. We met the production manager in the foyer. As we walked toward the door, I spotted a framed black and white photo of the "big house" under the pipelines.

Thinking to start laying the groundwork, I nodded to the photo and said, "Most people would expect the root of the problem to be in there." The production manager pulled open the door, "Just as well we dropped it then."

As we stepped out onto the yellow-lined pavement, I tried to process what he'd said. We turned the corner and I saw that he was right. There was nothing ahead except the pipelines, cooling towers, and a two-tone expanse of tarmac, darker and fresher in the distance where something had once stood.